For Selina

# For Selina

*Sandra Wynn*

iUniverse, Inc.
New York Lincoln Shanghai

**For Selina**

iUniverse, Inc.

For information address:
iUniverse, Inc.
2021 Pine Lake Road, Suite 100
Lincoln, NE 68512
www.iuniverse.com

ISBN: 0-595-28291-1

Printed in the United States of America

# Contents

## *Part VI*    *The mid 20th Century*

# Introduction

It was not until my father, Charles Arthur Wynn, died suddenly in February 2000 that my sister Janice and I realised that there was so much about our ancestors that we did not know. Our mother, Kathleen, had died just two years earlier and the shock of losing both of our lovely parents in such a short time was almost more than either of us could bear.

Janice decided to put down what little information we knew onto a genealogical computer programme, and after that there was no stopping either of us from searching for more. This was just the therapy we needed to help us overcome our terrible grief.

This research has since become a labour of love as it keeps the memories of both our parents and grandparents fresh in our minds. We are amazed at what we have found out and what our parents did not know, or more likely, what they were not told.

We have both spent many hours in record offices all over the country, have visited numerous churches and graveyards, made extensive use of the World Wide Web for information, and I have spent many hours on the phone speaking with numerous relatives, renewing several old acquaintances and making lots of new friends.

Janice and I have often enjoyed days out doing our research and sometimes visiting the Family Record Centre, which is situated in Islington, London, close to where one of our ancestors, Cornelius, used to drive his hansom cab. Our journey from Victoria to Islington on a number 38 bus, takes us past St Giles in the Fields Church, where our great grandfather, Charles John, and his sisters, Sarah and Phoebe, were all married. I could go on listing the city churches, the walks around the West End of London and St Pancras that I have taken to see the various places our ancestors lived and worked in, but there are too many.

The diaries my mother kept from 1957 until five weeks before she died in 1998 were one of our sources of information. As a child I can remember her saying that these were private and none of us should read them and we never did.

I read the diaries soon after my father died and as well as the information they contained, they made me even more aware of what a complex character my mother was and how very fragile her state of mind could be at times. They also showed me how very happy she had been in her marriage, but I feel sure that although my father did not destroy the diaries after she died, he would have honoured her wishes and would never have read them.

During all this frantic research, our husbands have shown remarkable forbearance. On some evenings, Janice and I would talk to each other on one phone line while we were both connected to the Internet on our other line, often for hours at a time. Our research has always been a joint effort, so this book would not have been possible without my dear sister and her input.

The research would probably have stayed just that—research, had it not been for the arrival of my granddaughter, Selina, who was born in Spain in July 2001. I realised that with her growing up in Spain, she would be unlikely to hear very much about her English Heritage. When she was a year old I had the idea of writing a book especially for her, about the life and times of our ancestors, and this is the result.

There are four people I would like to include in this introduction for various reasons. Bob, my husband, who has encouraged me to write this history of our family and corrected my grammar; Janice, my sister, who did half of the research and often stopped me getting carried away with ideas; my Uncle Les, the last William Wynn, who has given me such a lot of information about my grandparents, even though I had to coax it out of him; and my cousin, Maggie Reynolds, whom I had not met since I was a child, for sending me lots of valuable old Wynn papers, for relating many Wynn family anecdotes to me, and for becoming my close friend until she died in August 2002.

My husband has told me for years that I had "a book in me" and the history of our ordinary English family seems to me to be the perfect subject.

# *Prologue*

✦

## 25<sup>th</sup> *July 2001*

The phone rang at three in the morning. Your grandfather answered it and I could hear one side of the conversation he was having. It was almost non-existent, but I immediately knew what it was about. He said, "Talk to your mother, she'll tell you what to do" and handed me the phone.

The call was from your father, Stuart, who two years earlier had decided to live and work in Vila-Real, Spain, so that he could marry your mother, our delightful Pili. He had given up quite a lot to do this, as he had a job working together with us in our language school in Eastbourne. At the time he decided to leave, he was successfully marketing for us and travelling all over the world. Your grandfather and I had both looked forward to him taking over more responsibilities of our business in the future, but he decided that his future happiness was with Pili in Spain.

We were all eagerly awaiting your arrival, but not for at least two more weeks. Your parents had just moved into their new home and still had a lot of things to do, but you would not wait any longer to join this family. In the middle of the night, Pili's waters had burst although not much else was happening. Were you on the way? What should he do? The questions were flying down the phone line from Spain. "Go to the hospital, don't panic, drive carefully" was my answer. I wished them good luck, lots of kisses and put the phone down.

Ten minutes later and by then very wide-awake, I just had to call them back. They were still at home sorting out their dogs and were just about to leave for the hospital. They already knew that somehow I would get to Spain that day. I reassured them I would be there as quickly as it was humanly possible and would let them know my travel plans later in the day.

Of course, sleep was out of the question so I decided to try to organise my journey. You cannot imagine how easy it is to make travel arrangements at four o'clock in the morning. I knew the times of the flights to Valencia because I visit Vila-Real so often—too often, some might say. That night I contacted the British

Airways website and had my flight booked within minutes. I only had to make one phone call to give them my credit card number and my seat was confirmed on the lunchtime flight to Valencia. I then organised a car though Avis, who also take bookings all night, so by five o'clock that morning everything was booked and I was ready to go.

There was no point in going back to bed, as I was too excited to sleep, so after ironing at five thirty in the morning and tidying up the whole house, which actually wasn't untidy, I got ready and took the train from Polegate to Gatwick Airport.

I had not heard another word from your father in Spain during all this time, so I really hoped that I was not flying out on a false alarm. At last, at eleven o'clock that morning, he called me to say that nothing much more had happened and if things did not start again soon, the doctor would give your mother something later in the afternoon to help you on your way. He also wanted to know where I was and was very pleased to know that I was waiting to board my flight. I was on my way to meet my granddaughter.

Valencia is one the easiest airports to get around, especially when you fly in and out of there as much as I do. As I only had hand luggage, I collected my hire-car, was quickly out of the airport, drove like a demon to Vila-Real and headed straight for the new Hopital de la Plana.

Your father had obviously worked out exactly when I would arrive and as I drove into the car park the first thing I saw was your other grandmother, Pilar, waving her arms and calling me. This was really fortunate, as I had no idea where I had to go and Spanish medical terms are not my strongest point. We hurried straight to the maternity department where your grandfather, Juan, and Aunt Yolanda were patiently waiting. They had no news, there was no sign of your father, but at least things had progressed since I had last spoken to him while I was in Gatwick airport. Things were obviously happening because he was in the delivery suite with your mother.

We sat for about five minutes and then the doors of the delivery suite opened. Your father proudly wheeled you and your mother out to us. His first words to me were "I knew you'd be here Mum".

Our beautiful Selina had arrived.

This book is for you—it is the story of your English heritage.

# Part I

## The late 18<sup>th</sup> Century

✦

### *Wynns and Ravens*

# 1

## *The Wynns*

### WILLIAM WYNN AND ELIZABETH MARTHA GASS

Our family story starts in the spring of 1799. That year there had been a really bitter winter with a late spring, which had been one of the coldest for many years. George III was King of England and had not yet gone mad, although he had managed to lose the American Colonies. England was at war with France, where the monarchy had been deposed, and Napoleon Bonaparte was preparing to become the First Consul.

Imagine our William Wynn, a small man, who lived in the Lower Thames Street area of London, on his way to his marriage to Elizabeth Martha Gass at St Giles Cripplegate Church, which is now in the centre of the Barbican in the City. He would have been wearing his winter greatcoat, as an icy cold wind would without doubt blow in from the Thames, and Elizabeth would almost certainly be wearing her best, or maybe her only winter dress. There would be very little money to spend on materials to make new clothes, as both the Wynn and Gass families appear to have come from the working classes.

In 1799, the population of the City of London was about 70,000. The city was the richest part of the capital, which together with Westminster had a population of about 1.4 million. The population of the whole of Great Britain was only 9,168,000 when the next census was taken in 1801.

Both William and Elizabeth lived in the city before their marriage, Elizabeth having been born there in September 1779 and baptised three weeks later at St Luke Old Street, Finsbury, her parents were John Gass and his wife Elizabeth whose family name was Workman before she married. Elizabeth Workman may not have been her natural mother as she did not marry John Gass until two years after Elizabeth's birth but on Elizabeth's baptism record her mother is named

Elizabeth so her mother's ancestry is a bit of a mystery. Her father's parents came from the Finsbury area and were named John and Martha Gass.

William's birthplace is unknown; although it may well be that he came from Nutfield in Surrey as the following extract has been taken from the London City Apprenticeship records.

*Wynn William, son of William, Nutfield Surrey, blacksmith (deceased) to Richard Green, 11 Jun 1770. Farriers Company*

If this is his apprenticeship it would make William about thirty-nine years old at the time that he married.

Family legend always claimed that the Wynns originally came from Wales and as a child I was told that for many generations my Wynn ancestors had always worked with horses, so it could be that William Wynn the blacksmith, or one of his forebears moved from Wales to Surrey. It seems to be quite reasonable to think that our William is the same person as the apprentice particularly as Wynn was not a common name in London at that time, and to have two William Wynns who worked with horses seems quite unlikely.

One thing I do know about William, is that he was able to write his name. This was uncommon for one of the working classes, but he could have been taught this during his apprenticeship. His signature is quite clear and well written on his marriage licence, and his name is spelt without an 'e' on the end.

His ability to write leads me onto another possibility that he could have been an illegitimate son of the Williams-Wynn family who came from Gwydir in North Wales. Three of the members of this family were Members of Parliament for Denbighshire, so they would have spent time in London, and for three generations their names were Watkin Williams-Wynn. Our family called one of their sons Watkin, in each successive generation for the next one hundred years, but this is all pure conjecture and just adds to the mystery of his ancestry.

I have found another William Wynn who was baptised at St Paul's, Covent Garden in June 1778 and this could also be our William as he would have been twenty-one in 1799. This William Wynn was the illegitimate son of Catherine Wynn who was born in 1759 in Covent Garden, her parents being William and Catherine Wynn. As you can see I still have a lot more researching to do.

Back to William and Elizabeth who were married by the Vicar of St Giles Cripplegate, Reverend G.W. Hand, on 31$^{st}$ March 1799 after obtaining a licence from William's parish church, St Magnus the Martyr. This was one of the many city churches built by Sir Christopher Wren. By 1799 it was one of the landmarks of London, as anyone approaching from the River Thames could see its tower. The church formed part of the approach to London Bridge remaining as such until 1831 when the new bridge was built. Today, although St Magnus the Martyr has no parishioners as it is surrounded by office blocks, it is a well-maintained church and somewhere peaceful to go for prayer and contemplation.

# Exact Copy of the Vicar General's office licence.

## Dated 27 March 1799

*Which day appeared perfonally WILLIAM WYNN and made oath that he is of the parish of Saint Magnus the Martyr London a Batchelor of the age of twentyone years and upward*

*And intendeth to intermarry with ELIZABETH GAFS of the parish of Saint Giles Cripplegate London a spinster of the age of twentyone years upward*

*And he knowth of no lawful impediment, by reafon of any per-contract, confanguinity, Affinity, or any other lawful Caufe whatfoever to hinder the faid intended Marriage, and prayed licence to folemnize the fame in the Parish Church of St Giles Cripplegate aforesaid*

*And further made Oath that the ufual Place of Abode of her aforesaid ELIZABETH GAFS hath been the faid parifh of Saint Giles Cripplegate for upwards of four Weeks laft paft*

*W WYNN (signature)*
*Sworn before me*
*C COATE (signature)          Furr*

Exact Copy of the Marriage Register of St Giles

Cripplegate

*William Wynn of St Magnus the Martyr London Bachelor and Elizabeth Gass of this paris were married in the church by licence this 31st day of March 1799 by GW Hand Vicar. the marriage was solemnized between us William Wynn and Elizabeth Gafs in the presence of John Fowler and P Berry.*

Elizabeth Gass was twenty-one years old at the time of her marriage and I have already calculated that William was about thirty-nine, but I may never establish that for certain. I am sure that William worked with horses, but do not know much about Elizabeth although at that time many young women of her class went into service until their marriage. In those days once people married children usually arrived in quick succession, so it would be likely that a wife would take in washing or clean the homes of the middle class merchants who lived in the city. The lucky few that were taught plain sewing would be able to keep their family on what they could earn by sewing for the gentry, but most working class women had to do menial tasks for very little reward.

William and Elizabeth had at least four children, the oldest being our ancestor John Thomas Wynn, who was born in 1800 in the City of London. Their next child, William, was born in 1803 followed by two daughters, Sophia and Caroline, who were born in 1807 and 1808 respectively. William, Sophia and Caroline were all baptised in St Giles Cripplegate so the family obviously still lived in the city. These younger children are not mentioned again in this family history, as we have only been able find a record of their births. I have been unable to trace any of them any further in any of the city church records so I have assumed that they died in infancy or childhood, which was very common at that time.

There is so little information on our William and Elizabeth that their shadowy figures pass out of our family story at this point. However, the name William has been used in every generation of the Wynn family until the last male Wynn was born in 1928. We will rejoin the Wynn family later in this story with their son John Thomas.

# 2

## *The Ravens*

### JOHN RAVEN AND ELIZABETH RIDGEWAY

The Raven family originally came from Buckinghamshire, and for many generations they worked as agricultural labourers. The family first lived in the Parish of Wing and then some of them moved across the fields to Waddesden. It is here that I have traced a direct line to our ancestor Joseph Raven, who was born around 1630. I have also found many more Ravens who lived in Wing, as far back as the early sixteenth century when church records were first started by the order of King Henry the Eighth. The name Raven has been spelt in several different ways in the parish registers, including Reuing and Rauen, but this is probably due to an illiterate parish priest rather than the family changing their name.

Waddesden, which is a pretty village with a lovely church, was recorded in the Doomsday Book as being the largest estate of a Norman Knight. In the mid-eighteenth century it was mainly a farming community, but the Enclosure Acts ensured that by 1815 there was very little common land, causing the agricultural labourers of that time to suffer extreme poverty. The village became known as 'Black Waddesden' as bull baiting, dog fighting, cock fighting and other cruel pursuits were commonplace. Strangers passing through the village were often subjected to physical and verbal abuse. In 1830 there were riots in the village, when workers destroyed the new machines, which they felt, were being introduced to replace them and therefore they would lose their natural right to work on the land. At this time, two local charities financed the emigration to America of 88 young people from Buckinghamshire, including some from Waddesden. They travelled from Aylesbury on the Grand Union Canal to Liverpool where they embarked for a new life. Although many died on their way to America, the Raven family have descendants there to this day.

Waddesden remained an agricultural village and in 1874, the De Rothschild family bought many acres of the surrounding farmland and built a large manor house in the style of a French château. This created a lot of extra work for the villagers and many more houses were built, which completely changed its character. The National Trust now owns Waddesden Manor and it is a lovely place to visit.

John Raven was born in 1791 in Waddesden. He came from a widespread family with brothers, sisters and many cousins, who all lived in the surrounding area and worked on the land as agricultural labourers. In those days, without any form of transport available, the Raven family would have considered it normal to walk the few miles across the fields to the neighbouring village of Wing where many of their relatives were still living.

John married a widow called Elizabeth Ridgeway and they had at least six children who were all born in Waddesden. Elizabeth, who was baptised in Waddesden in June 1793, came from a local Waddesden family and had six brothers and sisters.

Her father, who had come to Waddesden from Oxford, was named Pilgrim Ridgeway. He was a religious man, and he wanted her to have the same sort of life, so when she was nineteen he insisted that she marry one of her cousins called William Ridgeway.

Unfortunately William died soon after they were married and she was left a childless widow. She then went into service in the nearby parish of Puttenham in Hertfordshire and it was here that she met John Raven. They were married in Puttenham in April 1814 and returned to live in Waddesden again.

The children of John and Elizabeth were Thomas, who was born in 1814, and Mary, Sarah and Joyce who followed in 1817, 1822 and 1825 respectively. The chances are that there were other children born between these dates but they were probably stillborn. In 1828, our ancestor John Raven was born, followed by their last child, a girl named Herodias, in 1831.

Surprisingly the Raven family often gave their children uncommon names and apart from Herodias, we have also found other ancestors called Alice Kingham and John Wallington. In later generations there are Corelenia, Levi Tennant, Moses, Amadine, which somehow became Hamerdine a generation later, and your namesake, Selina, a name that has once again become quite fashionable.

John and Elizabeth did not have a long marriage as he died in 1834 when he was only forty-three. He was buried in Waddesden churchyard and although I have searched the cemetery thoroughly, I was unable to find any trace of his grave or any graves of earlier Ravens who were also buried there.

Can you imagine the hardship of his widow, Elizabeth, who still had very young children to bring up? In that era, when so many infants and children died of starvation, and in a village with as many social problems as Waddesden had at that time, this would have been all the more likely to happen in a family with no husband and father to support them. Sadly it would appear that only Thomas, Joyce and John survived to adulthood.

Although there had been generations of the Raven family living in Waddesden and Wing for many centuries, Elizabeth and her family left 'Black Waddesden' in the 1840's and moved to Bushey in Hertfordshire so that she and her sons would be able to find work. The family were eventually to move to Watford, where some of their descendants are still living today.

It is quite likely that some of the Raven men from Waddesden went off to fight the French in the Napoleonic Wars and probably did not return. The rest of the family either died out or moved from Waddesden and Wing, and consequently there are no members of the Raven family currently living in either village.

I was next able to find the widow Elizabeth Raven in the 1851 census, when she was living at Flint Hall, Bushey in Hertfordshire with her youngest son John. This sounds like a grand address, but it was in fact a row of labourers' cottages very near to Bushey Railway Arches and close to Chalk Hill, which is one of the main roads leading into Watford. At that time the cottages were surrounded by fields, but now the area is built up. The cottages no longer exist, having been pulled down around the turn of the twentieth century. Most of the men living in Flint Hall Cottages worked in the local ironworks, but Elizabeth's son, John Raven, remained an agricultural labourer throughout his life.

Elizabeth reached the grand old age of 70, which was unusual in the mid-nineteenth century. She was listed in the 1851 census as a match-woman living with her youngest son, John, and her eleven year old grandson, William, who was Thomas's son.

I will tell you a little more about her surviving children, who although they are our ancestors, were not our direct line.

Thomas, her elder son, who was also a farm labourer, moved to Neales Yard in Watford, close to his sister Joyce, who had moved there when she was widowed. Thomas married and had a son who was named William, and was born in 1840. I believe that Thomas's wife died in childbirth, as it appears that his mother, Elizabeth, took care of the child while he continued to live alone in Neales Yard. Thomas died in Watford in 1894.

Joyce, who was the only surviving daughter, married Thomas Stratfield in Tring in 1847 and the couple made their home in that village. They had five children but only two of them, James and Maria, survived to adulthood and Joyce was soon to be widowed. She then moved to 2 Neales Yard in Watford, where, to make ends meet, she let out her rooms and became a lodging housekeeper. Our ancestor Anne-Maria Raven, who was also her niece, later married one of her lodgers called Henry Aldridge.

Elizabeth continued working and looking after her grandchildren until she died which was after 1851 but before 1861. With her death I end the first part of our family history.

Keep on reading, Selina.

# PART II
## The early 19<sup>th</sup> Century

✦

*Wynns, Ravens and Groschs*

# 3

## *The Wynn's*

### JOHN THOMAS WYNN AND ANN PLUMB

Eighteen months after the marriage of William Wynn and Elizabeth Martha Gass their son John Thomas Wynn was born on 14th October 1800 in the City of London. He was baptised when he was six weeks old on 23rd November at St Luke Old Street, Finsbury. He appears to be the only child of William and Elizabeth Wynn to survive the perils of an early nineteenth century childhood. After John Thomas grew up, he moved from the city, preferring to live and work in the West End of London.

John Thomas married Ann Plumb, when she was twenty-two years old, at St James Church Paddington on 22nd September 1823, and although he could not sign his name on the marriage register, she was able to sign hers. The witnesses to their marriage were John and Sarah Palmer who will never appear in our family history again. Unfortunately I have never been able to trace Ann's family in London so I think she may have come to London from the country, and was probably a servant when she met John Thomas. I have found three 'Ann Plumbs' who were born in the right period, from Ormskirk, Chipping Norton and Northampton, but I am still no wiser about her parents or origins.

John Thomas sometimes called himself a veterinary surgeon and at other times a farrier, so it is clear that he worked with horses and carried on what we think is the Wynn family tradition. He did not appear to have an apprenticeship, so he probably learnt his trade from his father William.

During the early years of their marriage, John Thomas and Ann lived in Berners Mews, St Marylebone. Berners Mews still exists and the old mews buildings, which had once housed the servants and retainers like John Thomas and Ann, are now the goods entrances to shops and offices. The mews are situated just behind the north side of Oxford Street, at the Tottenham Court Road end, and are overshadowed by the Post Office Tower. In 1966, Berners Mews was used as a set for the popular BBC children's series "Doctor Who".

It seems that John Thomas and Ann Wynn were extremely fortunate, as most of their children survived to maturity. Ann Elizabeth, who was born in 1825, went into service when she was about fourteen and I have discovered that she later married Henry James Kennedy in Stepney.

Watkin and Eliza, born in 1827 and 1830 respectively, lived until at least 1841, but there are no later traces of them. However, I have found another Watkin William Wynn of about the same age, who also lived in London at this time and worked as a railway clerk. He apparently came from another branch of the Wynn family that was from Painswick in Gloucestershire.

Their next son, John, who was born in 1833, became a confectioner and lived at home with his younger brother, William John, after their parents had both died. Another son, Thomas, who was born in 1838, was a labourer who lived all his life in Marylebone. He married, but I have no record of his wife or of when he died, but he was still alive when the 1881 census was conducted.

William John Wynn, who was our ancestor, was John Thomas and Ann's last child, and was born on 10th April 1840 in Berners Mews. Not long after William John was born, the family moved to Little Charles Street, Grays Inn and then to Cottage Place, Grays Inn. William John grew up in Cottage Place and lived and worked in the St Pancras area of London all throughout his life. Some of his descendants continued to live there until 1976, although most of them moved away after their homes were bombed in World War Two.

When William John married Sarah Dilley, his older brother John moved to Brighton. John boarded with a hansom cab proprietor, named Edward Jeffrey, in Blackman Street and continued to work as a confectioner. He does not appear to have returned to London again and as there is no record of him marrying he probably died alone in Brighton.

John Thomas and Ann were both alive in 1851 and like most of the population of London at the time, would have taken their son William to see the Crystal Palace of the Great Exhibition in Hyde Park. They would never have imagined that eighty-five years later one of their descendants would stand and watch it all burn down.

Ann Wynn died of bronchitis in Cottage Place St Pancras when her son William was fifteen. His father, John Thomas, did not outlive his wife by very long and he also died of bronchitis two years later in 1857.

# 4

## *The Ravens*

### JOHN RAVEN AND ANNIES PEARSE

Flint Hall, Bushey was a poor but fortunate community, where the men went to work in the ironworks or the fields and the women went into service where and when they could.

John Raven met Annies Pearse when she moved into one of the cottages with her mother, Caroline Pearse. They lodged with a farm labourer named James Hopgood whom Caroline later married. Caroline originally came from Northamptonshire, where she had met William Hyde who was Annies father. He did not marry her and she had Annies baptised in St John the Baptist Church, Boddington, Northampton in May 1825 before once more travelling around.

Caroline was a skilled needlewoman and when her daughter Annies grew up she became a hawker. They had walked from Northampton to Watford, a market town where they could easily sell their needlework.

Annies name is spelled in so many different ways throughout her life but I decided to use the first one I came across. We also found her called Anice, Alice, Ann, Anis, Anince and Annie.

Once Annies met John Raven, she decided she was going to travel no further. John was twenty-three and Annies three years older when they married in St James, Bushey Parish Church in August 1851 and settled into Flint Hall.

Their first children, Cornelius and Olive, were born in 1852. Although Olive died young, Cornelius survived to later marry and have two sons called Arthur and George. The next children of John and Annies were David and Anne-Maria, who were born in 1855. David never married and was a farm labourer all his life, but Anne-Maria's story will be told in another chapter, as she is our direct ancestor.

John and Annies moved to Watford in 1856 where there were more opportunities for work. James and Caroline Hopgood also moved to Watford with them, but we are not sure about John's mother Elizabeth who may have died some time after 1851 in Bushey.

The whole family made their home in Ballards Buildings in the centre of the town, and remained living in that area for the rest of their lives. John continued to work as an agricultural labourer, but although Annies was busy having babies she still found time to work in the paper mill at this time, so Caroline took care of the children for her. Life was very hard and there was not always enough food to go around their ever-growing family, so Annies would make sure her children ate before she did.

Levi Tennant was born in 1857, and although he later married a woman known only as Elizabeth, they had no children. He survived until the ripe old age of 80 and collapsed and died in the street in Watford from a heart attack. At the time, he was still working for Watford Urban District Council as a night watchman. Caroline and Coralenia were born in 1860, but both died before their first birthday. Fortunately the next baby, Selina, who was born in 1861, was healthy and strong. After attending school in Watford, she then went into service with Tom Coleman Ginger, a butcher of Stanmore in Middlesex. Selina married Jesse Carpenter, a maltster from Watford, when she was twenty-six years old. She then moved back to live in the same part of Watford as her parents and had at least five children.

John Albert was Annies's next child. Born in 1864, he became a sewerage labourer and married Elizabeth Walker. Once again they stayed living in the same area, in one of the many yards and alleys around Farthing Lane. In 1901 they had a daughter who was born in Red Lion Yard, Watford. Here was yet another Selina.

John and Annies's last two children were named Moses and Amadine. Moses was born in 1865 and died of marasmus, which is prolonged starvation, when he was nine months old. Amadine was born in 1867, when Annies was forty-two, but she also died in her infancy.

John and Annies appear to have been a very happy couple and they remained extremely close to all their children and most of them stayed living in close proximity to their parents. They also brought up another Moses, their grandson, of whom you will hear more in future pages.

In February 1902, after over fifty years together, Annies became ill with bronchitis and two weeks later she died of exhaustion in Ballards Buildings. She had lived for 83 years, which was a considerable age in those days, particularly as she had given birth to so many children in what were very poor living conditions.

John only lasted nine months without her, dying from a cerebral embolism in November of the same year.

# 5

## *The Groschs*

### JOHN GROSCH AND HARRIET CLARKSON

An adventure, which was to last his lifetime, was just starting for young Johannus Grosch. Johannus, who lived in Mainz, Germany, was to go to England with his two elder brothers, George and Wilhelm who was a tailor.

I have not been able to trace how the brothers travelled to England, but it is likely that they travelled down the River Rhine to Rotterdam and crossed the North Sea to England on a ship that was probably going on to America. These ships were overcrowded and insanitary, but fortunately two of the Grosch brothers would have disembarked before conditions got too bad. They may have landed at Deal on the Kent coast or in Deptford in London. They would have probably avoided travelling through France, which was in the midst of a revolution at the time.

When the three brothers arrived in England, George, who was the oldest, appears to have stayed on board the ship and travelled on to America where he founded the American Grosch family line.

Wilhelm and Johannus immediately anglicised their first names becoming William and John Grosch, as both had decided to stay in England for the remainder of their lives. In England, William made a great success of his career eventually being offered an appointment as a tailor at the court of Edward, Duke of Kent, the father of Queen Victoria. He stayed at court, where Germans were always very popular, as a tailor, was a member of the Guild of Clothiers, and became a Freeman of the City of London. He married an English girl called Kate Eliza, and had three children, Alfred, John and Elizabeth. His descendants live in England to this day.

John Grosch, who is our ancestor, was born in 1784 in Mainz, Germany and also became a tailor like his brother William. We are not sure exactly when he arrived in England and, as he did not have a court appointment, he set up his business in the West End for wealthy Londoners and became very successful. He seems to have been a level headed man who knew exactly what he was doing. When he was twenty-five, he married Harriet Clarkson at St Georges, Hanover Square, Westminster, which still remains an extremely fashionable London church. John had married well as Harriet came from an affluent London family.

John and Harriet lived in a large house in Francis Street near Tottenham Court Road, they had seven children and John was a very good provider for his family. Harriet may have had a hard life giving birth to at least seven children, but she lived in relative luxury with servants to take care of her. The children all had settlements made on them and the girls who chose not to marry could live very comfortably.

John and Harriet's oldest son, William Henry, appears to have been his father's favourite son. He also became a successful tailor and worked in St James's Place, Hampstead Road. William Henry had nine children and some of his descendants still live near London, but his wife died in 1852 when his youngest daughter Caroline was only seven. In his old age William lived at the Balls Pond Road Metropolitan Benefit Society and died of senile decay at Islington Infirmary in 1889

The second son, John, lived for seventy-six years and also had a son, but we know nothing else about him. George Grosch, our ancestor, was his third son. He was born in 1816 and we will learn more about him in a later chapter.

Mary, who was born four years after George, chose never to marry and spent her time visiting various parts of the country including a visit to Okehampton in Devonshire in 1851, where she lived as a boarder of independent means. The next child, Harriet, who was born in 1822, died aged twenty.

Harriet's younger brother, Charles who was born in 1827, became a Gas Fitter and married Sarah Parkes. Charles and Sarah had ten children but in 1869 when he was only forty-two, he died in Marylebone Workhouse from cerebral softening and paralysis. The last of John and Harriet's children was Charlotte, who died aged twenty-three.

John Grosch was a very successful London tailor and as a result of this, it enabled him to be initiated as a Freemason in the Royal Athelstan Lodge No. 19 in 1825. Four years later, he became the Worshipful Master of the Lodge and remained a Freemason until 1853—just two years before he died. He is recorded in the Masonic history books as having received a silver snuffbox on the 11th January 1843 as a tribute of the high esteem the members of the Royal Athelstan Lodge felt towards him. The following year he presented the Lodge with a case to hold the Masonic glasses belonging to the lodge. Usually a snuffbox is only given to a Freemason who performs an absolutely word-perfect ceremony, so we can be justly proud of our ancestor who could achieve this rare feat, particularly as English was his second language.

We know very little more about the life of the family although they continued to prosper. John and Harriet appear to have remained on close terms with their children, as his will shows. Harriet Grosch died of natural causes at her home in 1841 and Charlotte, their unmarried daughter, died the following year. For the rest of his life, John appears to have lived alone in the house with his servants, but his unmarried daughter, Mary, was probably with him for some of the time. He made his will in 1853 and became ill a year later, he lived on for one year and died in February 1855 of natural decay. His son, William Henry, was at his side.

## Copy of the will of John Grosch.

*I JOHN GROSCH of no 5 Francis Street, Tottenham Court Road in the County of Middlesex Tailor hereby revoke all Wills Codicils and other testamentary dispositions at any time heretofore made by me and declare this to be my last Will and Testament. I direct that my debts and funeral and testamentary expenses shall be paid as soon as conveniently may be after my decease. I bequeath the goodwill of the business of Tailor now carried on by me in Francis Street aforesaid and also the stock in trade cutting board and all other said implements used in my said business and of which I may be possessed at the time of my decease unto my eldest son William Henry. I also bequeath to my said son William Henry the silver snuff box and the silver Jewel or Medal presented to me by the Royal Athelstan Lodge of Freemasons which I request at will regard as heir locum. I also bequeath to him the portrait of myself painted by Mrs Forster and the Iron Safe or Chest in which I keep my Account books. I bequeath to my son John my other silver snuff box. I bequeath to my Son Charles my silver watch (by Samb) half a dozen silver tea spoons (to be selected by him after my daughter Mary shall have selected the half dozen hereinafter bequeathed to her) my wardrobe and body mirror. I bequeath to my granddaughter Alice the daughter of my eldest son William Henry my silver Geneva watch (by Jarol) and the silver curb guard chain attached thereto. I give and bequeath to each of my sons William Henry, John, George and Charles the sum of Ten pounds each to be paid to them as soon as conveniently may be after my decease. I give and bequeath to my daughter Mary the following articles of household furniture and other effects namely all the bed linen pillows blankets and counterpanes of which I may be possessed at the time of my decease. The mahogany dining table and mahogany chest of drawers with mahogany handles which I purchased of Mr George Bot, the best fender and fire irons now in my parlour, the set of eight old fashioned mahogany chairs with hair staff, the round mahogany pillar and claw table, a washhand stand with fittings, six silver teaspoons, two silver table spoons and all glass and china and all table linen and towels of which at the time of my decease I may possess. I also give and bequeath to my said daughter and hereby direct that she shall be at liberty to select from the household furniture and effects belonging to me at the time of my decease such bed mattress and bedstead, such out of my pier glasses, such out of my swing dressing glasses, such out of my stocks such pictures not exceeding four, such books and also all such kitchen utensils as she may think fit. And I direct that the rest of my household furniture goods and chattels fixtures and effects not hereintofor disposed shall be sold with liberty for any of my said children to purchase the same or any part thereof at a fair valuation and I hereby declare that the proceeds of such sale shall sink into and form part of my residuary estate hereinafter disposed of and I give and bequeath all the rest residue and remainder of my estate and effects not heretofore disposed of to my sons William Henry Grosch and John Grosch and my friend Samuel Galt of No 320 Oxford Street, Ironmonger my executors hereinafter named upon trust to get in and convert the same into money and out of the same provide for and pay to my said daughter Mary the sum of six shillings weekly and every week for the period of six months after my decease and I direct that the first of such payments shall be made at the expiration of seven days after my death and upon further trust to lay out and invest the remainder my said residuary estate after providing for such weekly payment to my said daughter as last aforesaid in or upon such stocks, funds or securities or in such manner as they my said executors may in their discretion think fit. And I hereby declare that my said sons William Henry Grosch and John Grosch and the said Samuel Galt and the survivors and survivors of them and the executors, administrators and assigns of such survivor shall stand and be possessed of and interested in my said residuary estate and the stocks, funds and securities in or upon which the same shall be invested upon trust to receive the interest, dividends and annual product thereof and pay this same by weekly payments unto my said daughter Mary during her life for her own absolute use and benefit and after her decease I direct that the said residuary estate and the stocks funds and securities in or upon which the same shall be invested shall be equally divided between my said sons William Henry, John, George and Charles and I hereby further declare that my said son William Henry may at the discretion of his coexecutors and upon giving to them such security as they may deem satisfactory have the use of my said residuary estate to assist him in carrying on the business he paying interest for the same after the rate of four pounds for every one hundred pounds by the year and I appoint my said two sons William Henry Grosch and John Grosch and the said Samuel Galt Executors of this my will with full powers and authority to compound debts and adjust all claims against or in favour of my estate and retain to and reimburse the monies respectively all costs charges and expenses which they or any other of them sustain or be put to in the execution of the trust of my will.*

*The writing whereof I have hereunto set in hand this fourth day of January One thousand eight hundred and fifty three-John Grosch-published and declared by the said Testator John Grosch as for his last will and Testament in the presence of us who in his presence at his request and in the presence of each other have hereunto subscribed our names as witnesses-Samuel Burch Barnet-Harriet Ellen Charleston.*

# NOTES ON OTHER GROSCH'S

Some of the information on the Grosch family was supplied to me by Kathleen Grosch of Milton Keynes, who is married to Leonard, a descendant of John Grosch's younger son, Charles, who died in the workhouse. Kathleen has done a tremendous amount of research on the Grosch family, and I am grateful to her for being so generous with her findings.

When John Grosch made out this will, he did not mention three of his children, who were still living and who Kathleen had found and attributed to him. Although I have done some research myself, I cannot find the proof that they are his children. This makes me suspect that they were not in fact his children, but the children of either his brother William or maybe even other immigrants from Germany with the same surname. These are the children in question:

Jacob Grosch who was born in 1825 and married Wilhelmina Wagner, who also had German blood. He became a telegraph wire worker and lived for part of his life in Drury Lane, London. Jacob and Wilhelmina had five children and their descendants are also around to this day.

Leopold, who was a coal merchant living in Manchester, was born in 1826. He married, but his wife died young so for some unknown reason he left all his money, which was over two thousand pounds, to a William Henry Renshaw.

Julius Hermann who was a watchmaker and was born in 1831. He also married an Anglo-German called Annie Hocklesoner.

# Apart from our branch of the family, John Grosch and his brother had some descendants of which they would have been very proud, including:

Monsignor Henry James Grosch 1860-1923
A senior priest in the Catholic Church

Charles Henry Grosch 1880-1916
Died in Action at Cambrin France

Albert Edward Grosch 1886-1917
Died in Action at Bethune France.
*Awarded the Military Medal for his brave actions*

Alfred Grosch 1888-1955 A Writer and Philanthropist.
*His book St Pancras Pavements was published in 1947*

Charles Joseph Grosch OBE 1901-1976
A Physician and Surgeon

John Thomas Grosch 1910–1942
Royal Pioneer Corps Died in Action

James Edward Grosch 1913-1998
A semi-professional boxer

Henry Alexander Grosch 1935-?
A Bank Director in Colombia
*He was kidnapped by FARC and never seen again*

# PART III

## The mid 19<sup>th</sup> Century

◆

*Wynns, Ravens, Groschs, Stacks
and Sheldricks*

# 6

# *The Wynns*

## WILLIAM JOHN WYNN AND SARAH DILLEY

We are now coming to that part of our family history where there are ancestors who were known to some of our older living relations, so at last we have more accurate information and know a little more about their true characters.

William John and Sarah Wynn and their family are some of my favourite ancestors. There really is no reason for this, apart from the fact that they were almost the first ones I discovered and I feel that they were a wonderful family who were full of love and affection.

Our first Victorian ancestor was William John Wynn who was born at 25 Berners Mews St Marylebone on 10<sup>th</sup> April 1840. This was the year when Queen Victoria married Prince Albert of Saxe Coburg Gotha and the first adhesive postage stamps, the Penny Black and Twopence Blue, were produced. William John was to outlive Queen Victoria's reign by twenty years, surviving into the reigns of King Edward V11 and King George V.

Unfortunately for William John who was the youngest son of John Thomas Wynn, his mother, Ann, died when he was only fifteen. William John followed in both his father and grandfather's footsteps, as a horse keeper and ostler. He worked with horses and lived in the various mews, within close proximity to them for most of his life.

William John was to see many changes in his lifetime, including the first trams in 1861, the underground railway in London and the first internal combustion engines, which propelled the horseless carriages. These introductions contributed towards the end of our family's long involvement with horses.

In 1862, when he was twenty-two, he married Sarah Elizabeth Dilley at St Mary Magdalene Church in St Pancras. She had been born in Pleasant Garden, Islington in about 1837 and was the oldest daughter of Charles Dilley, a fireman at the gasworks. She came from a large family of thirteen children and like her future husband, William John grew up in St Pancras. Sarah was at least two years older than William and was in domestic service when they met.

After their marriage, which was reputed to be very happy, William John and Sarah lived in a mews house in Little Charles Street, Grays Inn. Sarah worked for most of her married life as a charwoman, only stopping to have her babies. This must have been a great help with the family income, as until they moved into Keppel Mews, William John often seemed to change his job and this also involved moving to another mews cottage.

Neither William John nor Sarah had been taught to write their names and could only put their marks on their marriage certificate. This seems very strange for William John, when two generations earlier his grandfather had been able to sign his name in a clear script. It is not clear whether William John's father, John Thomas, was able to read and write, but his mother, Ann, could only make her mark on his birth certificate, although she had previously signed the register when she was married. William John and Sarah certainly educated their children and they all attended school when they were young.

The year after their marriage in 1863 William John and Sarah's first son, William Charles, was born; sadly he died of tubercular meningitis when he was four years old.

1863 was the year when the Prime Minister, William Ewart Gladstone, opened the first section of the London Underground. The line ran from Paddington to Farringdon Street in the City so it was more than likely that there was a lot of disruption in the area that William John and Sarah resided as a considerable amount of earth had to be removed by horse drawn carts from all the tunnelling and excavations.

Sarah Ann Wynn

William Charles's sister, Sarah Ann, was born in Churchway, St Pancras in 1865, and she is the first Wynn to be in a photograph. Sarah Ann, who was a parlour maid in her teens, married James Richard Embleton, a plumber and scaffolder, at St Giles in the Fields in 1884. James and Sarah Ann had thirteen children and their descendants include the Slingsby family, who are descended from their daughter Phoebe, and who are still carrying on the Wynn blood if not the name. Sarah Ann's last child, Maggie May Embleton, was born in 1903 and has a story all of her own, which I will elaborate on later.

Phoebe Wynn

When Sarah Ann was three years old, Thomas John was born. Unfortunately we have no further record of him, so we must assume that he also died as a baby. The next child of William John and Sarah was Phoebe, who was born in Christopher Place, Somers Town in 1870. Phoebe, who also went into service at fourteen, later married James Henry Collins at St Giles in the Fields in 1888. James Henry Collins was a furniture dealer's carman, but later became a glassware packer. Phoebe and James had four children and have many descendants who are our distant cousins. James, who did not have very good health, died when he was only forty-four. Four years later in 1911, Phoebe married Oliver Evans, a widower, whom she had known for many years and although they were happy together, he did not always see eye-to-eye with Phoebe's children.

The two sisters, Sarah Ann and Phoebe, were always very close and we always think of them as the first 'Wynn Girls'. A hundred years later another two sisters, Sandra and Janice Wynn, were the second set of 'Wynn Girls'. These are your grandmother and your great aunt.

Back to the 19th century now and to William John and Sarah. In the 1870's, their living conditions must have been a bit overcrowded as they had two of Sarah's brothers living with them in the mews cottage in Christopher Place. This leads me to believe that Sarah's parents were dead by this time. Sarah's brothers were named Charles, who worked as a fireman at the gasworks like his father, and Alfred, who was at school.

After William John and Sarah's daughter, Phoebe, was born in 1870 another son, Watkin Alfred, was born in 1873, but he died of bronchitis aged 2 years. It seems impossible to imagine the misery his mother Sarah must have felt at losing yet another son, but infant mortality was still high towards the end of the nineteenth century, especially in the area where they were living. She was probably able to accept it, as so many other families, living around her had to do the same in those days.

Their next child was our ancestor Charles John, who was born in 1875, after the family had moved yet again to Torrington Mews, St Giles in the Fields. Charles John had one younger brother, Alfred, who was born in 1879, and whom I think was the last child of William John and Sarah. Alfred was alive in 1901, but I have no idea when he died. He served in both the in Boer War and the Great War and I am not sure if he was one of the many who were known as 'cannon fodder' and did not return.

After Alfred was born, William John and Sarah moved to Keppel Mews near Tottenham Court Road and at last they seemed to settle, as this remained their home for many years. Keppel Mews was in the parish of St Giles in the Fields, which at this time was an area of great poverty and squalor with over 30,000 inhabitants. Fortunately the Wynn family lived away from the worst part, which was near to the church and was known throughout England to be the place for beggars, pickpockets and rogues, and had one of the highest infant mortality rates in the country.

Their children, Sarah Ann, Phoebe and Charles John, went to school, in all probability to the St Giles National School in Endell Street, which was opened before the Act for Compulsory Education was passed. The children were also married at St Giles in the Fields.

Sarah became ill with bronchitis when she was sixty-four and although Phoebe and Sarah Ann nursed their mother, she could not withstand the damp conditions and died in Keppel Mews with Phoebe at her side in November 1898.

William John was still working as a provision merchant's horse keeper at this time and he invited, his son Charles John, together with his wife and family, to move back in with him. He lived with Charles John and his family for the rest of his life, eventually moving with them to Bridgewater Street, St Pancras.

William John was the only Wynn male at home during the Great War, and it would have been his daughter-in-law Annie, who took care of him in his last years, even though he kept working as a carman until he died. He outlived his wife for many years and died of senile myocarditus in hospital at 4 Kings Road St Pancras, in 1922 when he was eighty-two years old.

4 Kings Road, St Pancras was the site of the old St Pancras Workhouse and in 1855, the St Pancras Union Infirmary was built here for chronic, infirm and bed-ridden patients.

Some of our earlier ancestors died in the workhouse and a few were also born in the hospital. I jokingly call it our ancestral home. Kings Road had a bad reputation because of the workhouse and at sometime during the early twentieth century the road was renamed Pancras Way, the hospital is still there.

The children of Sarah Ann, Phoebe and Charles John all grew up together, a great horde of cousins, who by this time were all living in St Pancras. The cousins were all great friends, but two in particular, Maggie May Embleton, who was the daughter of Sarah Ann Wynn, and James Ernest Collins, who was known as Ernie, the son of Phoebe Wynn, fell in love. Of course, both sets of parents opposed the match and there was a lot of family opposition to a marriage between first cousins, and it is now against the law for them to marry. Ernie was quite a gentle person, which is a typical trait of the Wynn men, but Maggie May was not, she had a very strong character, which even her daughter Maggie found rather overpowering at times. She was determined to marry her Ernie and even threatened to elope. In the end, they got their way and were married at St Pancras Register office in 1924. They had a long and happy marriage, which only ended when Ernie died in 1950.

Ernie and Maggie had only one child, perhaps because they were worried about the consequences of having more when they were so closely related. Their daughter was Maggie Florence Collins and she was a very special person, so full of life and energy and with the most loving nature. She married Tom Reynolds and went to live in Queniborough, Leicestershire after the Second World War, where she worked as a cook in the local village school. Maggie had one son, known as Young Tom, and two grandchildren she adored called Samantha and Gordon. Maggie, as she was known to everyone, used to joke about being the daughter of cousins. She often said that she had no sign of the inherited madness that is spoken about when close relatives marry and have children. She joked because the village she lived in was called Queniborough, and it was here that the mad cow disease epidemic, BSE, was discovered in the 1990's. Maggie died of leukaemia in August 2002 and is sadly missed by her husband Tom and her family and also by her many Embleton, Collins, Slingsby and Wynn cousins.

James Embleton with his granddaughter
Maggie Collins
The Granddaughter of both Phoebe and Sarah

Another of Sarah Anne's granddaughters is Kathleen May Embleton, who is always called Kitty. She was the daughter of Sarah Anne's son Alfred, who fought in the Great War at Mons and Ypres as a machine gunner. Kitty and her husband Sydney Hale, who is a member of the Salvation Army, have celebrated over sixty years of marriage. Although in their eighties, Sydney and Kitty, who live in Enfield in Middlesex, were still arranging holidays for the elderly, until June 2002, bringing at least one group of them to Eastbourne each year. Most of the group who came to Eastbourne in 2002 were younger than them. Kitty and Sydney have a son, daughter, four grandchildren and one great grandson. Kitty used to take your great grandfather Charlie to school when he was a small boy, but I only met her for the first time in June 2001 during one of her visits to Eastbourne.

# 7

# *The Ravens*

## ANNE-MARIA RAVEN

Anne-Maria Raven, who appears to have been a lively friendly girl, was born in Flint Hall, Bushey on 7th April 1855. This was the time of the Crimean War and of the great nurse and reformer Florence Nightingale, who was endeavouring to introduce higher standards of nursing and hygiene in the Crimea.

Unlike most girls of her social class, Anne-Maria did not go into service when she was fourteen, but was allowed to stay at school until she was over sixteen years old. It seems that, as she was John and Annies's oldest surviving daughter she was indulged by her parents. This does not appear to have done her any good as when she was seventeen, she gave birth to an illegitimate son at her parent's home in Farthing Lane, Watford.

This was not unheard of in this era when very little could be done about birth control, in fact it was very common for babies to be born within a few months of many marriages, but there was no wedding for Anne-Maria. This was a matter of great shame to her parents, John and Annies, and was destined to become a family secret for over one hundred years.

On the 28th January 1873 Anne-Maria gave birth to her son, Moses, but did not name his father. John and Annies decided that they would bring Moses up as their own son, while Anne-Maria would go into service. This was a great waste of all the extra education she had been given, but in an age when children, even in their late teens, did as their parents told them, poor Anne-Maria who had brought such shame on her family had little choice.

By 1881, Anne-Maria was living at Edgwarebury Farm, Edgware Middlesex, acting as a housekeeper and servant to Frederick Atkins, a farmer and labourer. Moses, her son, was at school in Watford and still lived with his grandparents. It seems that most of the family assumed Moses was the son of John and Annies, although she would have been forty-nine when he was born, and it is doubtful that Moses was told, even as an adult, that Anne-Maria was his mother. In fact he may never have known.

Anne-Maria embarked on a liaison with Frederick Atkins during her time at Edgwarebury Farm, which was probably inevitable as there were just the two of them living in the house. Regrettably she did not learn from her earlier mistake and became pregnant once again. It would appear that Frederick was not the marrying kind, or maybe he did not want to marry his servant, because once again she gave birth to another illegitimate son. Frederick Raven was born in December 1884 at Edgwarebury Farm in Edgware and was given his father's first name but not his family name. This appears to have been the end of her relationship with Frederick Atkins as she soon returned to Watford with her baby.

Anne-Maria's life may well have been a very bitter one. Although she kept her second baby, she seldom saw Moses and had nothing to do with his upbringing. It is doubtful that she ever found any short-lived happiness.

After Anne-Maria returned home to Watford with her baby, she met Henry Aldridge, a farm labourer, who was lodging together with his brother, with her Aunt Joyce in Neales Yard. Henry was eighteen years older than her and had never married, but he was willing to marry her and take on her baby son. This was probably Anne-Maria's only chance to escape from being a servant for the rest of her life and they were married in Watford Register office in November 1886.

Unfortunately within a year Anne-Maria was living in Watford Union Workhouse where she gave birth to her third son, whom she named Henry after his father. Her children, Henry Aldridge and his half brother Frederick Raven were baptised together at St Mary's Church in Watford on 25th November 1887 and Frederick was given the name Frederick Riven Aldridge in the parish register.

What happened to poor Anne-Maria? After her marriage, I cannot find any other information about her. I do not even know where she lived in Watford, or if she ever left the workhouse alive. If she did survive, it is quite likely that she moved into one of the many yards and alleys around Farthing Lane. This is where John and Annies and most of their children had their homes, so it must have been a nest of Ravens. None of the buildings or addresses where the Ravens lived now exist, and the main street, which was called Farthing Lane, is now known as Watford Field Road.

I suspect that Anne-Maria could have either died in childbirth, or very soon after her son Henry was born. She certainly died before 1891 as together with husband Henry Aldridge and her son Frederick, all three are missing from the national census returns. At the time of the census, her four-year-old son, Henry, was living with his grandparents, John and Annies, in Clarks Buildings in Watford, together with his cousin Moses, who was really his half brother.

# 8

## *The Groschs*

### GEORGE GROSCH AND MARY BOLT

George Grosch, who was the third son of John and Harriet Grosch, was born in Francis Street, St Pancras in 1816.

This was a time of economic depression in England following the end of the Napoleonic Wars. Although still very agricultural, England was becoming a manufacturing nation and had stockpiled goods that could not be sold in Europe due to the long wars that had impoverished her continental neighbours. This had not affected the Grosch family, in fact his father John probably benefited as the 10% income tax was abolished.

George was a professional hairdresser and had lived and worked in Maddox Street before he married. It was here that he met Mary Bolt, who was living in Hanover Square where she was a visitor, as she did not have any occupation when they were married. Mary Bolt had been born in Cheriton Bishop in Devonshire in 1814 and was the daughter of a gamekeeper called John Bolt.

George Grosch married Mary Bolt at St George's Hanover Square in 1841. At that time the second Afghan War was being fought and it was in this year that Britain started to rule Hong Kong. Queen Victoria's empire was growing.

George and Mary's first home was in Mansfield Place, St Pancras and their first son was born here.

They soon moved and made their home in Mortimer Market, a tiny square just off of Tottenham Court Road, and it was here that George opened his own hairdressing shop and worked hard to build up a successful business.

George and Mary had seven children between 1842 and 1858 but George did not survive to see them all grow up. Not long after their last child was born, George became ill with phillicosis, which is a lung disease that leads to asphyxiation and death. He was soon unable to work, so he gave up his business moving together with his family to 6 Warren Street where he died aged only forty-five in September 1861. Mary was left, a widow, with seven children to support.

Mary became a widow in the same year as Queen Victoria, but unlike the Queen she could not hide herself away to grieve, as she had no time or money for such luxuries. She never remarried and remained alone, bringing up her children, with no option but to work, and for the rest of her long life she toiled as a laundress.

The family soon moved from Warren Street to less expensive accommodation in Netley Street, St Pancras, where Mary managed to bring up and educate her children.

The oldest two boys, George aged nineteen and Reuben who was fifteen, had jobs as a porter and a paperhanger respectively, so they were probably able to contribute a little to the family income. George later became an oil artist and colourman, he married Martha Burgan, and had six children and many descendants. His wife outlived him for many years taking over his work and running his business when he died, she remarried in 1892. One of George and Martha's children Albert Arthur carried on the family tradition and became a tailor, opening a business in London Road, St Pancras.

Reuben became a French Polisher and married Sarah Ann Jones, they had seven children but he also died at the relatively young age of 44, his wife remarried two years later.

George and Mary's oldest daughter Selina was born in 1848, and when she was twenty-five she married an upholsterer named Robert Grant. Selina and her husband made their home in Netley Street near to her mother. It is highly likely that Selina's children would have attended the same school in Netley Street as the Wynn family children were destined to do early in the next century.

Mary's next son Frederick married Eileen Higginson and became an oilman and a house painter. They had three children and moved to St Marylebone then eventually lived at Queens Park, which is near Willesden.

George and Mary's next child was our ancestor Alfred Arthur Grosch, who was born in 1853 in Mortimer Market. After Alfred Arthur, the next child was his sister Teresa, who married in 1878 when she was twenty-two. Her husband was a blind pianoforte tuner called William Hall and they only had one child, a daughter who was also called Teresa.

They called the last of their seven children Herbert Henry and he was born in 1858. He also became an oil manager and lived with his mother in Netley Street until he married in 1888. Herbert Henry actually married two sisters, Mary Jane and Elizabeth Hayes. With Mary Jane he had four children but only one lived and Mary Jane eventually died in childbirth in 1893. Two years later he married her sister Elizabeth and they moved to Castle Road, Kentish Town, where they had five more children although two of these also died at birth.

Herbert Henry left one hundred and seventy three pounds to his wife when he died in 1929 and she outlived him by many years, dying in 1944 aged 77.

Having outlived several of her children, the widowed Mary Grosch died in 1908 at St Pancras Infirmary from nephritis.

The Grosch family in London had grown beyond all expectations from the two brothers William and John, who had come from Germany, and both lines seemed intent on producing more and more children.

What is an oil and colourman? I have made so many guesses, one Grosch claims to be an oil artist, so perhaps he painted pictures, another was a house painter, another owned a shop, and another was an oil colour manager. I can only assume that the main work was making and mixing paints, and that the Grosch's used the various paints according to their own abilities.

# 9

# *The Stacks*

## GARRETT STACK AND BRIDGET BROSNEHAN

It has been very difficult to find out any real information about our early Stack family, as the only member who is left alive will not open her front door and speak to me, even though she is my godmother. You will see as you continue to read this history that they were an eccentric lot and many would say 'barking mad'. As you will discover, a 'crazy' gene is very noticeable in some of the descendants of our family. However it does not come from the gentle Wynns, the strong-minded Ravens, or the industrious Groschs.

The Stack family appear to have originated in Ireland in the county of Kerry, which many Irishmen call the 'Kingdom Of Kerry'. Some were also found in Tipperary, although I do not know whether they were the same family. The surname is still found in Tipperary, but it was in Kerry that the family name became well known in the middle ages and is probably the reason for the name of the Stacks Mountains in the north of the county, approximately ten miles from Castleisland. By the seventeenth century the family were among the major gentry, and there were so many branches that the surname was soon found in the neighbouring counties of Cork and Limerick.

We start with Garrett Stack, who was born in Ireland in 1832. He was educated in Ireland and was probably brought to England some time during the eighteen-forties, by his father, Thomas, who was a soldier. Thomas was later given an army pension, which in those days was a Chelsea Pension. This income was enough for him to live very comfortably, so we assume he must have been an officer and therefore was likely to be a member of the Stack family from Kerry.

Garrett and Thomas came to England at the time of the Irish famine, which started in 1845 and continued for the next ten years. This famine caused the death of over 750,000 people. Although many thousands died, Kerry did not suffer as badly as most other counties in the Great Famine, with a drop in population of 19% between 1841 and 1851.

There were two main causes for the famine, a potato blight which turned the potatoes into a soggy smelly pulp before they could be harvested and the failure of British government to do anything to alleviate the suffering.

It was not just the failure of the potato harvest that caused the problems. Most Irish peasants' diet consisted mainly of potatoes and there were too many absentee English landowners, with no interest in their tenants, who rented out plots of land that were not large enough for the families to survive on without the potatoes.

In 1847 the government at last took some action and set up soup kitchens and some emergency relief. It was too little and too late as there was not enough money in the English Exchequer to pay for this. Over two million of the Irish peasants ended up in overcrowded workhouses where many of them died.

Another two million people left Ireland during this time, emigrating to America, Canada, Australia and about 100,000 Irish immigrants came to England. Many of them settled around London and there were several areas that later became known as 'Irish Nests'.

Garrett married an Irish girl whose name was Bridget Brosnehan, in December 1854 at St John the Evangelist Catholic Church in Islington. Bridget, who was twenty when she married, was an immigrant from Killorglin in Kerry and was the daughter of Daniel Brosnehan and Nora Leyne. She had a younger brother named Cornelius and named her son after him.

Garrett became a builder and labourer and the family made its home in Islington where Garrett worked. Garrett and Bridget were not too concerned with the laws of their adopted country and do not seem to have bothered with the registration of their son Cornelius, who was born within a year of their marriage. We believe they had other children, as there are several families of Stacks in addition to that of Cornelius, who lived in Quinn buildings in Islington in the late nineteenth century, but none of them appear to have been registered at birth.

Bridget had a short hard life and Garrett was with her when she died of an epileptic fit that lasted for twenty-four hours, she was just forty years old. Garrett never married again and lived in lodgings at Eden Grove, Islington after his son Cornelius left home, it must have been a sad and lonely existence. He stayed working as a builder in Islington until he died of phthisis in Islington Infirmary in 1884; he missed the birth of his first granddaughter Rosina by just three months.

# 10

## *The Sheldricks*

### GEORGE SHELDRICK AND EMMA MARIA LAIDLER

Bottisham, near Cambridge, is a picturesque village and was the home of the Sheldrick family for many centuries. The Sheldrick men married local girls from Bottisham and Stow cum Quy and we can trace a direct family line back to William Shildrick, who was born in Bottisham in 1753. The men of the family were carpenters and wheelwrights and a William Sheldrick, who died in 1822, was the landlord of the Rose and Crown public house in High Street, Bottisham.

In 1837, George Sheldrick was born in Bottisham and he was baptised there at Holy Trinity Church on 21st May 1837. He was the son of James Sheldrick, a carpenter, and his wife Elizabeth, whose maiden name was Flack. He grew up in Bottisham but decided to go to London and take his chances there as a carpenter and wheelwright. George was a handsome man with very blue eyes and lots of dark hair, but he had a mean temper and was always a heavy drinker.

He spent a few years roistering around the town as he always had plenty to spend due to his being a craftsman with a good trade. However, he always spent whatever money he earned and did not think about the future. When he was thirty, he met Emma Maria Laidler, a tiny frail looking woman who made children's shoes. Emma managed to tame him a little and got him to the altar as they were married in St Pancras Church in 1868.

Emma was the daughter of John Laidler, a chair maker from Berwick on Tweed, who like his son-in-law had come to London to try to improve his life. After John arrived in London, he met Jane Scott, who had been born in Christchurch, Surrey in 1807. They married in 1839 and made their home in Rawston Place, Clerkenwell. Emma, their oldest child, was born there in 1840 and grew up with John and Joseph, her two brothers, and her sister Sarah who was listed in the 1861 census as an idiot. The Laidler family later moved to Brunswick Buildings in Grays Inn.

Emma was no match for the larger than life George and he treated her quite badly. She soon became pregnant and gave birth to a daughter Emily, who was retarded. A year later, a son William was born but he soon died. In 1872, Emma managed a successful pregnancy and gave birth to her only healthy child, Esther Annie, at her parent's home in Brunswick Buildings, where she and George had lived since their marriage.

Just over a year later, another daughter, Harriet, was born but she died at eight weeks. Eighteen months after Harriet's death came the birth of another son George, but this little mite also died within eight weeks. Both babies died of a debility from birth. These are the babies I know about, but there may have been others I have not discovered.

Emma was worn out from bringing so many sick babies into the world and although in 1875 George had at last found them their own home, she was too weak and sick to care. George had his work to do and could not take care of her, so she did not last much longer. She died of phthisis, alone, in Lambeth Workhouse Infirmary in March 1877, leaving George to care for her two small daughters.

George could not manage to bring up his two young daughters and work at the same time, particularly as both his and Emma's parents were dead and his only relatives lived in Cambridgeshire. Jane, Emma's mother, had been ill for several years with heart disease before her death in 1867 and Emma's father, John, died of bronchitis in 1875.

George found the situation impossible, as he had to work to keep his children. He decided that the only possible solution was to lodge with a well-to-do widow in Park Village, St Pancras. The widow was called Emily Dean and her husband Richard, who had been a mason, had left her comfortably off. She had an unmarried daughter, Emily, who was the thirteenth of her fourteen children and the only one to survive. George came to an arrangement for them to care for his children, Emily and Esther, while he worked.

The arrangement worked very well for George and in 1883 he asked Emily, the daughter, to marry him and was accepted.

# 11

## *The Sheldricks*

## GEORGE SHELDRICK AND EMILY DEAN

Emily Dean was a very striking woman of thirty years with bright red hair when she married George Sheldrick. She was the total opposite of George's first wife, the gentle Emma, being energetic and full of life. She lived until she was ninety-two years old.

Emily (Dean) Sheldrick in 1929

Emily was just what George needed to look after both him and his daughters, but whether he made her any happier than Emma is debatable. He is reputed to have beaten both of his wives, and his granddaughter, Rosina, who remembers Emily, told me that her grandmother had said, "he was a bad tempered old bugger".

George and Emily made their home in Arlington Road, St Pancras and by this time George had a business in Islington making wheels for hansom cabs. It appears that George's retarded daughter Emily from his first marriage died soon after they were married and they went on to have three children of their own naming their first daughter, who was born in 1883, Emily after her older half sister. The next child was Georgina Sarah born in 1885 and their son George was born in 1890. Georgina married George Love around 1923 and had a daughter Rosina, who is the source of much of this information. Rosina married Stanley Faulkner and had two sons, David and Norman, and five grandchildren.

Had he lived longer, George would have been proud of his son George, as he joined the 11th Battalion London Regiment (Finsbury Rifles) as a rifleman to fight for his country in the Great War. Unfortunately, he was killed in action on the 8th September 1918 just before the war ended, and was buried at Tincourt New British Cemetery, Somme, France in grave IX.A.20.

George Sheldrick had been a heavy smoker all his life and he did not live long into the twentieth century, dying in 1903 of tuberculosis and emphysema. Emily who was only fifty at the time of his death outlived him for many years but chose not to marry again. She was well loved by her daughter's children, her stepdaughter Esther Annie and her family, and the Embleton, Collins and Slingsby families, who all invited her to stay with them, and knew her as Nan. She spent a great deal of her time with the Wynn family in St Pancras and often went on holidays with them.

During the Second World War, she was evacuated to the country away from the bombs, but she did not like it there, so she walked over forty miles back to her home in St Pancras and walked in the front door as if she had just popped out for a pint of milk.

Just before she died she visited Ringwood in Hampshire, where her granddaughter Rosina still lives today, Once again she suddenly decided to go home to Crouch End where she was living with some Embleton relations and took the first train she could get back to London. I can just imagine her walking around Victoria Station, she was over ninety years old and still dressed like a Victorian in a long black dress and a bonnet. She decided to take a taxi from Victoria and gave the driver her address but for some reason he doubted her ability to pay and asked her to show him her money before he would take her anywhere. She was annoyed by his attitude and told him he was a cheeky bugger; she then threatened to hit him over the head with her umbrella unless he took her home. She got home safely and paid her fare.

This was one of her last expeditions as she died not long after this in 1944 and although she was no blood relative, she was very much a part of the Wynn family and deserves her place in this story for taming George Sheldrick, and for the affectionate way she was remembered by all of her extended family.

# PART IV

## The late 19<sup>th</sup> century

♦

*Wynns, Ravens, Groschs, Stacks
and Flynns*

# 12

## *The Wynns*

## CHARLES JOHN WYNN AND ESTHER ANNIE SHELDRICK

Charles John Wynn was born in February 1875 and was the third of the four surviving children of William John and Sarah Wynn. He had a happy childhood with his two older sisters and his younger brother Alfred. His sisters, Sarah Ann and Phoebe, both went into service when they reached fourteen years of age. Charles John started work as a plasterer's labourer and Alfred became a grocer's carman.

Charles John Wynn

Charles John, who was a tiny man and only just over five feet tall, also had a cast in one of his eyes. He was a most gentle and uncomplaining man and very well loved by his sisters and all his family. On Christmas Day in 1896, he married Esther Annie Sheldrick in St Giles in the Fields. This attractive London church is very near to Tottenham Court Road and, unfortunately, is now overshadowed by an enormous ugly office block named Centre Point. The church was only a few minutes walk from Keppel Mews where the Wynn family were all living.

Esther Annie Sheldrick

It seems a very romantic thing to marry on Christmas Day and older members of the family have told me that Charles John and Esther Annie had thirty years of happy married life.

Charles John and Esther Annie moved to Crescent Place after they were married and Esther Annie soon became known as Annie by everyone in the Wynn family and this is what I will call her from now on. Annie was also tiny, being less than five feet tall, but she more than made up for this in character. She was very fiery and lost her temper easily, but it was always over in seconds and she never hit her children or grandchildren. The only exception was in later life when she hit her son, William Alfred, over the head with a hairbrush for going to the pub.

Two years after their wedding, Charles John's mother, Sarah, died of bronchitis in Keppel Mews in November 1898. Fortunately, she had lived long enough to see Charles John and Annie's first child, Charles George, who was born in 1897. After Sarah's death, Annie became the matriarch of the Wynn family and remained so for the next fifty-three years.

In 1899, Charles John and his family went back to live in Keppel Mews with his father and his brother Alfred and it was here that their second son, William Alfred, was born. William John was now sixty years old and still worked as a horse keeper. He was the last of the Wynn men to work with horses, as when the twentieth century dawned fewer horses were needed for transportation, this changed the way in which many working class men worked and many of the jobs that had passed down generations from father to son now died out. The Wynn home in Keppel Mews was also demolished to make way for one of the main buildings of the University of London, which was built on the site.

After their son William Alfred was born, Charles John joined the Essex Regiment as Private 57648 CJ Wynn, and went to South Africa to fight in the 2$^{nd}$ Boer War. There is a picture of him in his army uniform and the cap badge is the one for the Essex Regiment. It would appear that he may have been at the relief of Mafeking, as his regiment took part in that campaign but unfortunately his army records are missing at the Public Records Office, as many of them were destroyed in World War Two when a bomb hit the building in which they were stored.

After Charles John left the army in 1901, the whole Wynn family moved to a house at 21 Bridgewater Street in Somers Town and stayed there for the rest of his life.

Charles John was very patriotic and he rejoined the Army going into the Pioneer Corps, which was then called the Labour Corps at the beginning of the Great War, His brother Alfred and his son William Alfred also joined the Labour Corps. They were all on active service in France and fortunately Charles John and William Alfred survived, but Alfred disappears from the family at this time and no one knows what happened to him.

A quote from one of the commanding officers, Captain G.S. Fillingham, in 1916 is as follows:

*"A typical pioneers job was this—be present under fire all day in support of the main attack. Then move forward and grab ground and dig trenches in so called no mans land under enemy fire at night. Go back before day break, sleep and start all over again. Casualties no object!"*

His oldest son Charles George joined the Queens Royal West Surrey Regiment and we will tell his war story in another chapter.

### 1914 in Somers Town, North West London
An outing of the men of the
Wynn, Embleton Collins and Slingsby families.
On the Lorry: 1st left Charles John Wynn,
2nd left Jack Slingsby, 1st right Alfie Embleton, 3rd right James Embleton.
In the road: 1st left William Alfred Wynn,
3rd left Dennis Embleton, 3rd right Charles George Wynn.

After the war, Charles John and William Alfred both came home and went back to their labouring jobs. These were the good years between the two wars and there were many happy family occasions. The whole family of cousins, Wynns, Embletons, Collins, and Slingsbys would go by charabanc from Stibbington Street to the coast for days out, and there were enough cousins to fill the charabanc. At Christmas Charles John always used to play his mouth organ and this was always part of the family entertainment.

Charles John and Jack Slingsby after the Great War

Charles John and his sons would often enjoy a night out at the pub and one night he was so drunk that he sat on the bed with his son William, took one of his boots off and one of William's, and did not notice what he had done until the next day. Quite what Annie had to say about boots in bed we don't know. The happy years were too few and Charles John, who his daughter-in-law Lillie described as an angel of a man, died suddenly.

It was bitterly cold just before Christmas in 1927 and Charles John had a very bad case of Erysipelas, which is a skin infection, on his face. It was so bad that he was admitted to hospital in Dartmouth Park Hill, which is an awful trudge uphill from Somers Town. He had received quite a few visitors, who all complained about the hill and the cold, when he suddenly took an unexpected turn for the worse and died of heart failure just four days before Christmas Day, which would have been his thirty-first wedding anniversary.

He was buried in St Pancras Cemetery.

Annie and her son William Alfred soon moved to St Georges Flats, which were just across the road from their house. These flats were being built by the St Pancras Housing Association to improve people's living environment, so were a model for the times. The courtyards had very impressive sculptures by the famous artist Gilbert Bayes, who was also responsible for the famous clock outside the front of Selfridges in Oxford Street. Bridgewater Street is now called Bridgeway Street and St Georges Flats, which are still standing, have been modernised and are now very desirable homes. Unfortunately, the sculptures are gone, having been stolen over the years, although there are a few displayed in the Victoria and Albert Museum. St Georges Flats remained the family home until William Alfred, Charles John's brother, died there in 1976.

St Georges Flats, until they were modernised, had open entrances and communal sewage pipes, so all the flats were connected to the same down-pipe.

William Alfred took care of his mother for as long as she lived, or should I say that she took care of him until she died. She was always busy, kept the home spotless, and especially enjoyed having her grandsons and all their young cousins around. This was a time when smoking was not frowned upon and she used to ask them all for a cigarette as she was a chain smoker. She was also a very good cook and one of her great nieces, Maggie Collins, used to go round on a Saturday just to have some of her liver gravy, even though she did not eat the liver.

William Alfred Wynn

Like his father, William Alfred was also a small man of about 5ft 2 inches and he also had a cast in his eye. He did not seem very interested in marrying and was happy living with his mother, doing his labouring job, going to the pub and getting together with his extended family, most of whom had moved away from St Pancras after the Second World War.

In later life Annie was always still very active and her grandson, William Leslie, remembers her lovely Christmas dinners. Her niece Kitty Embleton remembers how spotlessly clean her home was and how she always made everyone welcome, but she would not put up with any gossiping or backbiting among the cousins.

I can also remember her sitting in her chair in St Georges Flats, although I was only three years old when she died. She was fit and active until she was seventy-eight although in the last few months she had diabetes that made her go blind. She went into hospital in Great College Street for an operation from which she never recovered. I remember visiting her in hospital, as I was her only great-grandchild at this time. She died of diabetes and complications from her operation in July 1950 and was buried near her husband in St Pancras Cemetery.

William Alfred, her son, went on to surprise everyone. On November 4th that year he married a divorcee, Florence Furnish, who was a manageress of a provision merchants. Although he was fifty-one and she was fifty-three, they had a very happy time together for the next twenty-six years. Auntie Flo, as she was known, was a generous woman who often invited us to tea in Bridgeway Street on a Sunday. The street had been renamed in the 1930's. She would always give us winkles, salmon sandwiches and plenty of cakes.

William Alfred and Flo lived on the first floor with other flats above them and in the very cold winter of 1963, the sewage pipe froze just below their bathroom. This meant that every time someone in one of the four flats above them pulled a chain or emptied a sink or bath, the waste water could only go as far as their flat and would overflow into their toilet. Unfortunately on one occasion, both William Alfred and Flo had been out during the day and returned home to find the toilet overflowing with other people's sewage. The only possible way they could not dispose of it was to bail it out with a jug into their bath. It took three days before they could get a plumber with a blowlamp to come and defrost the pipes outside and then they had to bail out the bath. They had to put up with a terrible smell until their problem was resolved.

William Alfred, Uncle Will to me, liked a joke in common with all of the Wynn men and always wanted an "invi" to any family celebration needless to say he was always welcome. He died in 1976 and shortly afterwards, Auntie Flo went to Yorkshire to stay with her married daughter, and we have never heard any more from or about her.

# 13

## *The Ravens*

### MOSES RAVEN AND ADA ELIZABETH SMITH

Moses Raven, who was born in Farthing Lane Watford in 1873, had a happy settled life as a child. Although his mother was Anne-Marie Raven, he was brought up to believe that she was his sister and that he was the son of his grandparents, John and Annies, with whom he lived for all of his childhood. He thought that he had older brothers and sisters, but they were really his aunts and uncles. He also had several young cousins who were his playmates.

In those days, Watford was a market town surrounded by fields and farms and was still very agricultural. Even now, it still has a market in the centre of its enormous modern concrete shopping area.

Moses and Ada

In 1894 when he was twenty-two and working as a labourer, Moses married Ada Elizabeth Smith in Oxhey Parish Church. Ada was the daughter of David Smith, who had been a dairyman when he was young and was now a brewer's labourer. This particular branch of the Smith family originally came from Aldenham. Her daughter, Ada Hamerdine, remembered Ada as a very ladylike refined woman who kept a spotless and well cared-for home, especially when the family lived in Cardiff Road, Watford.

Moses at this time was calling himself Thomas and signed the marriage register, as Thomas Raven I have never been able to discover any reason for this so maybe he just did not like the name Moses. He also named his father as John Raven, so I feel quite sure that he did not know the truth about his parentage. For the rest of his marriage to Ada, Moses appeared to have used the name Thomas, except on his army records. He also used the name Thomas on his children's birth certificates, and this caused some confusion, as his youngest daughter Doris was never quite sure if he really was her father. Especially as in later life he reverted back to being known as Moses. I will continue to call him Moses throughout this history.

Moses and Ada moved into Clarks Buildings in Watford and started their family, eventually having six children. Ada Hamerdine was the eldest of their children and she was born in 1895. She married George Harding; she had seven children and numerous grandchildren.

Ada Hamerdine Raven

Their second daughter was our ancestor Lillie Violet, who was born in 1896.

Lillie Violet Raven

In 1898 Moses joined the Army Service Corps and went to South Africa, probably to Natal, leaving Ada at home pregnant with her third child Edith, who was born in 1899. She later married Henry Walker, had six children and many grandchildren.

Edith Raven

Moses was invalided home at the end of the Boer War and left the army in 1903, returning to a labouring job in Watford. It was during his time in the Army that he had his arms tattooed. On his left arm he had a 'sailor with a flag' and on his right arm were 'crossed hands' with 'true love' written underneath them. I am quite sure they would not have been very well received by Ada when he returned home.

Their next child Beatrice was born in February 1903 and I believe she may have had Downs Syndrome, as her sisters, who all called her Beattie, used to speak about her as if there was something that needed to be kept quiet. She died of measles when she was eighteen.

Beatrice Raven

Arthur Harry Raven

Moses and Ada's last two children were Arthur Harry born in 1905, and Doris Daisy Maud who was born in 1907 and lived until January 2002. Arthur Harry married Ivy Stevens and they made their home in Sutton in Surrey. They had two children, Dennis, who became a telephone engineer, and Barbara, a very pretty child who was so severely handicapped that she spent all of her life in an institution.

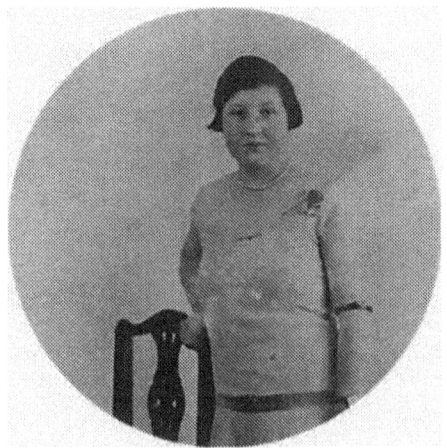

Doris Daisy Maud Raven

Doris Raven married Charles Cullum and had two daughters, Joan and Pat. Joan married Eric Roberts and had a daughter Annette and now has a grandson Lee. Pat the youngest daughter was my godmother, and I was a bridesmaid at her wedding to Don Smith in April 1959. Pat gave birth to a stillborn son in 1964 and the following year when she was expecting another baby was diagnosed with leukaemia and died a few days later.

I will return now to the early part of the twentieth century and back to the story of Moses and Ada. Their marriage was not a happy one and in 1914 Ada ran away and was never seen or heard of by any of her children again. She said "Goodbye" to her daughter Doris at Watford railway station, got on a train, and went out of all of their lives forever.

It was believed by many of her family that she had run off with another man, but this was never proved one way or another and it was certainly never spoken about. No one was ever able to find or trace her so Moses was left with five of his six children in his care.

Ada Hamardine, his first daughter, was by this time married and settled in Watford and that was where she stayed for the rest of her life. She told her daughters that she always felt sad because she never knew where her mother was, when she had died, or where she had been buried.

I have another theory about Ada, having spent many hours searching the records for her death. In the 1901 census, Moses and Ada were living at 14 Chapmans Court, Watford with their children Ada Hamerdine, Lillie and Edith, and at this time, they had two lodgers Henry and Herbert Raven, who I think were the cousins of Moses. Ada at this time was 26 and Henry was 22 and a brewery labourer, Moses was also away in the army around this time. I believe that twelve years later they may have run off together. I have no proof that this is anything more than speculation, but on 10<sup>th</sup> May 1954 an Ada Elizabeth Raven aged 79 died at 37 Vorley Road Tufnell Park. The death certificate names a Henry Raven, a builder's labourer, as her husband, who was in attendance at her death from cancer. The age of this Ada is correct, the job of Henry is the same and they were probably able to marry after Moses died, as although Moses never knew where Ada was, she may well have known where he was. Was this my great grandmother Ada? I will never know for certain.

Soon after Ada left her family, Moses and their five unmarried children moved away from Watford to St Pancras to live in Stibbington Street (now renamed Chalton Street), adjacent to Bridgewater Street, and so the Raven family became neighbours of the Wynns.

In May 1915, Moses, who was by now 41 years old, rejoined the Army Service Corps at Woolwich Barracks and strangely he gave his occupation as a miner. I have yet to discover any mines in the St Pancras area at that time. He named his daughter Lillie as his next of kin, stating that he was married to Ada but did not know where she was. He was discharged unfit a year later, having served as a driver in England.

Life for Moses changed at the end of the Great War and he soon settled down in St Pancras with a mistress called Beatrice. I am not sure whether she had been around in Watford but I think it is more than likely that he met her after moving to St Pancras.

It was at this time that he started to use the name Moses again. Much to the disgust of his children he and Beatrice lived together from this time until his death. They had four children but I have only been able to find out the names of three of them, Queenie, Trixie and Sonny, and these are probably just their nicknames. Unfortunately both of their sons died in childhood, Sonny of measles when he was about ten. I have been told that one of his daughters married, moved to Palmers Green and opened a shop. Whether there was a divorce after Ada had left, which was such an unmentionable thing in those days, is unknown but I think it is very unlikely, I have checked the divorce records at the Public Records Office and could not find any trace of one. I am still unsure if Moses was ever able to marry his Beatrice, but it is doubtful that he did. One thing I am sure of, divorce or not, they certainly tried to take all their secrets with them to the grave.

It appears that although his son and daughters by Ada Smith lived in the same house as him when they first came to London, they were all quite ashamed of him living with Beatrice and with the likelihood that they were never married. Lillie and Edith appear to have married from his home, but one of Ada Hamerdine's daughters told me that they had all lived a completely separate life from their father. When Edith married, Doris went to live with her, staying until her own wedding to Charles Cullum in 1930, which Edith had arranged. Once all the Raven children had left home, although they all lived in very close proximity to him, they appear to have had very little contact with Moses. His grandchildren seldom met him and therefore hardly knew him at all.

During his last years, Moses, together with Beatrice and their children, moved to a house in Bridgewater Street and he worked as a night porter in a garage. Like many men and women at that time, he was a very heavy smoker, a habit that he passed on to all of his and Ada's children. The smoking eventually took its toll and he died of emphysema and bronchitis at the relatively early age of fifty-eight. Arthur, his son, was with him when he died.

The rest of Moses' family ostracized Beatrice and her children and we do not know what became of them.

I am sure there is so much more to write about Moses and Ada, but whenever I ask questions I come up against the same comment from most of my elderly Raven relatives…*"We're not allowed to talk about that"*.

Moses, Beatrice, Queenie and Trixie

# 14

## *The Groschs*

## ALFRED ARTHUR GROSCH AND ELIZA JOHNSON

The Grosch Family of London had grown very large by the second half of the nineteenth century. Alfred Arthur Grosch and his wife Eliza were related to twelve other families of Grosch brothers, sisters and cousins of their generation. Based in and around North London, between them they had produced at least sixty-six children for the next generation. Most of the family were tradesmen and we have found house painters, a paperhanger and a woodcarver. One of the grandsons, Charles Henry, carried on his grandfather John's work as a tailor, and several others worked as oil artists and colourmen.

Alfred Arthur Grosch was born in 1853 in Mortimer Market, Saint Pancras, the fifth of seven children. His father died when he was eight years old so he probably had quite a tough childhood with very little money to go round. However, I am sure that his branch of the Grosch family never went without, as several other branches were rich and successful.

Eliza Johnson was a country girl and had been born in Redbourn, Hertfordshire. Her father, William, was a successful boot and shoemaker, as his father had been before him, with a business in Redbourn High Street. Eliza decided to come to London and became a nursemaid for the family of Dr George Lawson in Harley Street, which is now as it was then, the area for many doctors and private clinics. Dr Lawson had seven children and Eliza was one of several servants in the house at the time. They included a Nurse, Under Nurse, Cook and two housemaids.

Alfred Arthur, who lived in Marylebone at the time of his marriage, and Eliza were married in St Thomas's Church, Portman Square in April 1877. Eliza had never had to work after her marriage and her husband, Alfred, kept her in very comfortable conditions. The couple set up home in Gloucester Road, St Pancras and had six children.

Their eldest son, Alfred Lewin, opened a grocery shop at 341 Ladbroke Grove, which was very successful. During the Second World War the windows of his shop were smashed by some British men who thought he was a German because of the name above the shop. The whole family were very upset by this as several of the patriotic Grosch men had fought for the British and some had died in both wars. Alfred went to Somerset House and searched for his ancestors and is reputed to have traced them back even further than we have to a Grosch from the Netherlands, He then put a sign in his shop window listing his antecedents and this put a stop to the vandalism. When Alfred died in 1950, he left over four thousand pounds to his sisters, Ethel and Nellie.

The rest of Alfred Arthur and Eliza's children were Ethel, William and Nellie, and they were followed in January 1887 by what seems to have been the black sheep of the Grosch family, my grandfather Arthur Henry. Alfred Arthur and Eliza had one more child, their last son Frederick who was born in 1888.

Alfred Arthur was only thirty-eight when he died of acute heart failure in 1891. His youngest son was only three years old and his eldest, Alfred Lewin, was still only thirteen so I am sure this family also suffered many hard times, although they do not appear to be too badly off. Eliza's father, William, was still working at this time although four years later he died in St Albans Workhouse.

Eliza and her children moved to a large villa in Bathhurst Gardens, Harlesden, where she managed to bring them all up. Her grandson John told me she was a strict lady, who always dressed in the Edwardian style and was a very imposing woman. She did not approve of strong drink and her son, Arthur Henry would ask anyone who knew that he had been to a pub not to tell his mother. She was a widow for many years but was not alone, as her daughter, Nellie, never married.

When she died at the age of seventy-six, she left her oldest son, Alfred Lewin, one hundred and sixteen pounds in her will.

# 15

## *The Stacks*

## CORNELIUS STACK AND ROSINA DUNSFORD

Nothing is known of Cornelius as a child, apart from the fact that he was born in Islington. I think he may have had at least one brother, who lived near him in Islington, when he was an adult. His mother, Bridget, died when he was still in his early teens and he left home and became a servant as soon as he could. His father, Garrett, who lived until 1884 never married again so Cornelius must have had quite a lonely time after his mother died.

We first learn about Cornelius Stack and Rosina Dunsford when they met in 1881 while they were both working for Mr Theodore Stienkopff, a commission merchant, who lived in Cavendish Road in Willesden. Rosina was a general servant at the house and Cornelius went to work there as a temporary servant.

Rosina, who was born in Islington in 1860, was the daughter of Thomas Dunsford, a carpenter and joiner. In those days this was a good trade and Rosina was probably well provided for as a child. Her father, Thomas, who originally came from Exeter, had married Mary Pickering in Portsmouth in 1859. They then came to London and made their home in Islington. I often wonder what they thought about their daughter marrying Cornelius Stack.

Two years after they met, Cornelius and Rosina married in Islington Register Office in July 1883. They probably married with great hopes as most young couples do but and I am sure that at this time Rosina's life changed, doubtless for the worse. By the time of his marriage, Cornelius was working as a hansom cab driver, and this was his job for the rest of his life. Their first daughter, Rosina, was born in 1884 but died when she was twelve years old. Cornelius seems to have moved his family around the Islington area during much of his married life and we are not sure whether this was from choice, or as we suspect, perhaps they could not always afford the rent.

Their oldest son, Walter Cornelius, was born in 1887 in Alma Terrace, Islington and worked as a carman until the Great War, when he joined the 1st London Machine Gun Corps and served with distinction on the Western Front. The Corps actually went into battle for at least one hundred days during the course of the war, and at some stage Walter Cornelius was badly injured and lost one of his legs for which he received a medical discharge from the army with a full pension.

From that time on, he walked with a crutch and always refused to wear a false leg. He never worked again and was always supported by Margaret, his younger sister and my grandmother, until he died in Edgware in 1954.

Although Walter was a kind man at times, he was not so happy after his niece Kathleen left home to get married as he missed her very much. He was a bit of a frightening figure to his great nieces as he had a long white beard and in his old age, not very much patience with children. He used to grow one of his fingernails until it curled up like a snail's shell, and every few months he would get a bowl of hot water to soak it until it was soft enough to cut. Then, with a great deal of fuss, the nail would be cut off and thrown away. Although I did not like to go too near him when this great performance was taking place, it always fascinated me and I just had to watch. I was quite fond of my Uncle Walter and visited him right up until the time he died.

Walter Cornelius Stack
with Esther Sheldrick Wynn in 1946

Charles, their next son, was a year younger than Walter Cornelius and was a quiet man who never furnished much information about his life. When he left school he became a bakery rounds man and this was his job until he served in the Great War. Charles joined the West Riding Regiment in March 1916 and was sent to the Eastern Front. Fortunately he was not injured and returned from Dunkirk on 30th July 1919. He then learned a trade with a printer and after the family moved to Edgware in the 1930's, he spent the rest of his life running his own printing press from a shed in his sister Margaret's back garden.

As a child I loved to spend time with him in his printing shed, as he was a very gentle man. He would give me all the off-cuts from the paper he used and when he went dog racing in later life he always gave me a three-penny bit if he won. He died around 1958 when he was seventy years old.

I now have a bit of a puzzle, as Margaret, my grandmother, told me many stories about her brother Sammy, who died when he was young. She never said how he had died, but she used to get very sentimental about him. Although I was uncertain when he was born or how long he lived, long searches at the Family Records Centre in Islington at last revealed that he died of cancer in March 1925 when he was twenty-four years old.

Samuel Stack

This means he was born in 1901, but I have been unable to trace his birth certificate. He was Cornelius and Rosina's youngest son and was born when she was forty-one. I have one picture of him in a dress uniform when he looked about twenty, so I think he may have been a soldier in the Great War. I know that his brother Charles named him as next of kin when he joined the Army and he acted as a witness at his sister Mary's wedding in April 1923 but that is the full extent of my knowledge of him.

Cornelius and Rosina's last two daughters and the only ones to survive to adulthood were my grandmother Margaret who was born in 1894 and her sister Mary born five years later. The sisters often quarrelled throughout their lives but still remained close and kept in contact with each other. I remember Mary as a very stern but kind woman, and know that she had been married to a Charles Offord, but he had died before I was born. They had two children called Reggie and Mary and the family were dog lovers who always kept Alsatians. Her daughter Mary, who was the same age as my mother, is my godmother, but until a few years ago when I tried to visit her, I had not seen her for nearly forty years.

Reggie remained a bachelor all his life and lived with his mother until she died and then with his widowed sister, Mary, until his death. Mary who married Douglas Channel in the late 1940's never had any children. They moved to Long Stratton in Norfolk where Mary, who became a recluse after Douglas and Reggie died, is still living today. Although I tried to visit her several years ago, she did not want to talk to me and slammed the door in my face. This is such a shame as I would like to get to know her again and I am sure she could give me some more information about her parents and grandparents, but this is unlikely to happen. I still write her a letter every few months in the hope that she will answer me.

I will return to Cornelius and Rosina now despite there being not much more to tell. After living at many different addresses in Islington, Clerkenwell and Finsbury, Cornelius and his family eventually moved to Brewery Road, Islington, but by this time Cornelius was a sick man. He kept driving his cab until he was fifty-five when he was admitted to St Pancras Infirmary, where he died of tuberculosis in October 1912.

Rosina and her family moved again, to James Street in Islington where her son, Walter, who was twenty-five and working as a carman, became the head of their household. Rosina only outlived her husband by two and a half years and she died from exhaustion in 1915 after an operation at Islington Infirmary for a strangulated femoral hernia.

# 16

## *The Flynns*

# FROM 1823 TO 1900

This is a very short history of your grandfather's family and it will be little more than names and dates as I have been unable to ask any questions to any of the living Flynns, so all the information I have is based on research that I have done.

I have traced your grandfather Bob Flynn's ancestors back to Westminster, London in 1823, when John Peter Flinn married Elizabeth Rawlings. They had two children, a daughter Lucy, and your ancestor John Flynn, who was born in Westminster in 1831 and also died there in 1894.

In 1859 John Flynn who was a master builder and bricklayer married Lavinia Sims who had also been born in Westminster at St James's Westminster. John and Lavinia had five children, James, Mary, your ancestor John, who was born at 8 Cross Street Westminster in 1863, Charles and Ann.

The third John Flynn married Rachel Catherine Ray in 1888 in Enfield in Middlesex. Rachel, who was also born in Westminster, was the daughter of an American, Charles Ray, a modeller and master gas fitter, and his English wife Rachel Garrett. The Ray family lived in Maidenhead Grange, Westminster.

John and Rachel Flynn lived at 2 Hopkins Street, Westminster after their marriage. They had four children, Lillie, Daisy, John and the youngest, Alfred James, who was your great great grandfather. All I have found out about John is that he worked at various times as a printer and a warehouseman. Unfortunately I cannot tell you any more about Rachel.

I have no record of the deaths of John and Rachel or their children, Lillie, Daisy and John so this is where the early history of the Flynn family ends.

# PART V

## The early 20<sup>th</sup> Century

◆

*Wynns, Ravens, Groschs, Stacks*
*and Flynns*

# 17

## *The Wynns*

### CHARLES GEORGE WYNN—HIS EARLY LIFE

Charles George Wynn was born in Crescent Place, Tottenham Court Road in September 1897, the oldest son of Charles John and Annie Wynn.

The family then moved back to Keppel Mews after his grandmother died and it was here that his brother, William Alfred, was born. Charles George and William were both quite small as boys and had each inherited the cast in their eye. Even as an adult, Charles George was only five foot tall and when he joined the army at 18 his chest measurement was just 31 inches.

Charles George and William Alfred both went to school in Netley Street, St Pancras, which at the time was a boy's school. It is just off Hampstead Road and the school still exists today. Charles George won four medals for good attendance, one of which was The Kings Medal. It was awarded by London County Council for punctual attendance at school between 1908 and 1911.

Charles George Wynn in 1916

Charles George left school in 1912 and went to work for a large wholesalers company called R Hovenden and Sons in Berners Street, which was around the corner from the mews in which his grandfather had been born seventy two years earlier. He was employed in the perfumery and cosmetics department and he really enjoyed his job and soon became an expert on perfumes. Apart from two years war service, he stayed in this one job for the rest of his life becoming the Under Manager in charge of foreign perfumes.

On 15th May 1916 Charles George, who was nineteen, went to the Central London Recruiting Depot in Whitehall and joined the Royal West Surrey Regiment. He did his initial training at Sturry and Tunbridge Wells barracks in Kent and here he was given vaccinations and inoculations, trained in a gas chamber and completed a general musketry course.

Charles George at Ypres
2nd from the left

In April 1917, he was sent to France where he fought in the Battle of Messines in June, which was one of the most successful campaigns of the Great War. The British soldiers needed to take a ridge from the Germans as it gave such a good view of all the surrounding areas and overlooked the British positions This they did by exploding nineteen mines and bombarding the Germans with over three million shells from 2250 guns. This attack was a success and there were very few casualties. While he was fighting he developed a serious double hernia, which could not be repaired and he was supplied with a truss on 11th May 1917 while on the battlefield, and he had to wear one for the rest of his life.

Marching to Ypres with the 'Royal Surreys'
Charles George is the 6<sup>th</sup> soldier in the first row

He sent this postcard to Lillie from the trenches, the message on it was:

*Dear Lil*

> *Just a few of the boys as we marched into the town.*
> *We all look as if we have had enough of it.*
> > *With love*
> > > *Charlie*

During his time in France Charles George drew twenty-seven pounds five shillings of his army pay to use while on active service, which is the equivalent of about 40 euros in today's money. A lot of this went on postcards, postage and photographs that he sent home to his future wife, Lillie. He probably considered himself very lucky to be in the trenches during the summer months, although he would not have known how short his time in France would be, but 1917 had the worst summer since records began and by August the trenches were full of mud and water. His feet were constantly submerged in the filthy slime, which was often more than two feet deep and caused many soldiers on both sides to drown in this mire. The only possible way to move around was on duckboards. Just imagine here was Charles George fighting for his country, and for the liberation of the French, in a trench that could have been dug out by his father, brother and uncle.

Charles George was badly wounded in the third battle of Ypres when he took part in the Battles of Pilkem Ridge and Langemark in July and August 1917. His wounds were severe, he had bullet wounds in his right arm and leg and more serious wounds, caused by shrapnel in his stomach and back, from which he never completely recovered. While he lay in injured in the trenches he was with a German soldier who was even more badly injured, Charles George gave him a drink of water from his own bottle, but it did not help him and he died with only an injured Englishman to give him any comfort. Charles George was carried away from the battlefield on a stretcher by stretcher-bearers who saved him although they were under fire. One of the stretcher-bearers picked up a helmet and put it on Charles George's head to protect the only part of him that was not injured but this, unfortunately, was the helmet of the German soldier that had died, so Charles George kept calling out "I'm not a bloody jerry" to make sure he did not get shot by his own side.

He was operated on at one of the Casualty Clearing Stations, which had some qualified surgeons and senior nurses or matrons, but which were mainly staffed by "VADs" Voluntary Aid Detachment Nurses and "FANYs" First Aid Nursing Yeomanry. VAD nurses usually had about three months training in a hospital in England before being sent to the front lines. These nurses were patriotic middle class young women who believed that they should also be doing their duty, but they could never have been prepared for the suffering and injuries that they would encounter.

The rule on the battlefield was that no advancing soldier was allowed to assist an injured soldier. Each soldier was issued with emergency field dressing kits and had to try to treat their own wounds. Those who were more seriously injured had to lie in no-mans land and wait for stretcher-bearers, who also had to pick up the dead and take them to the graveyards. The stretcher-bearers even had to make the choice as to whether to carry some of the very badly wounded to the casualty clearing stations or the graveyard, where they could only look on helplessly as they watched them die. Conditions were terrible and as the ground was a quagmire, it sometimes took six men to carry a stretcher because of the depth of the mud and slime. During this time they were also in danger from German bombs and shells as the enemy deliberately targeted the stretcher—bearers and injured soldiers. It seems strange to imagine that if the stretcher-bearers carrying Charles

George had decided he was too badly injured to survive, none of us would be here today.

Charles George probably counted himself as one of the lucky ones when he arrived at the Casualty Clearing Station, although these were very near the front lines. The conditions here were filthy and about one third of all the casualties who were operated on died of either gangrene or septicaemia. A surgeon often worked on more than one patient at a time so cross infection was very common.

After his operation, Charles George was transferred to a field hospital by a horse drawn ambulance and we can only imagine the pain and discomfort he must have been in. From the field hospital, when he was fit enough to travel, he was transferred on one of the hospital trains back to Britain.

He was repatriated to the 3$^{rd}$ Scottish General Hospital in Glasgow where he was admitted on the 15$^{th}$ August 1917 with 60% disability, the hospital had room for 70 officers and 1629 other ranks. After his treatment was complete and he was fit to leave, he went to Troon in Ayrshire where he spent several months alone, recovering and convalescing, hundreds of miles from his fiancée and family. On his way to the hospital he had to pass through London, but had been unable to get any message to his family, although he was probably less than two miles away from them.

Charles George Wynn was given an honourable discharge from the Army, signed by King George, in 1918.

## Copy of his honourable discharge

*202458 Private Charles George Wynn*
*The Queens Royal West Surrey Regiment.*
*Served with honour and was disabled in the Great War*
*Honourably discharged 10th December 1918. signed George RI*

When he was discharged from hospital he returned to Tunbridge Wells barracks and from here, on the 22$^{nd}$ November 1918, he wrote to Hovenden and Sons to enquire whether his old job would be available. They obviously held him in high esteem because he received a reply within three days inviting him to resume his duties as soon as he received his army discharge. Charles George went straight back to work even though he was still unfit and suffered terribly for several months until he regained his health and strength. He probably thought this was the best thing to do as many men had returned from their army service to find no jobs available for them. Despite the severity of his injuries he only received an Army pension of 16 shillings and 6 pence, the equivalent of 1 euro, for 11 months.

Charles George was the first of the Wynn men to arrive back from the war and his father Charles John and brother William Alfred, who were both in the Pioneer Corps, did not return until early 1919. His uncle Alfred appears not to have returned at all.

Copies of two letters he wrote to Lillie when he arrived at the hospital in Scotland from the trenches at Ypres, the first one was written soon after his arrival when he was still very weak.

*My Dearest Lil*
*Just a few lines in answer to your loving letter which arrived safe. I am going on well. I am sorry I am so far away but that's just my luck but still I might get moved later on. We passed through London last Tuesday week. Dear Lil can you send the cigarettes and the chocolates as I am allowed to have them. Thank F. Anderson for the photo. I have just heard from J Scherer and he is going on well I think this is all for the presently. Best respects to All*
*From yours with love*

*Charlie XXXXXXXXX*
*Excuse writing left hand*
*send books*

*My dearest Lil*
*Just a few lines to answer your loving letter and to thank you for the books, which arrived safely. I am going on well and hope to be up in a few weeks but expect I shall have another operation with my arm. I had one in France. Am glad you are having a fine time and enjoying yourself but wish I were with you. Dear Lil don't forget the cigs as up here they cost double the price than they did in France and our issue this week has been 2 cigs (not many for me). We are having some lovely weather up here pouring with rain 1 minute and sunshine the next minute. We have just had a sample of it. Tell mother to tell aunt Emma I can have the eggs. Hoping this finds you and all at home in the best of health. With respects to all and EP*

*With best love from your loving sweetheart*
*Charlie XXXXXXXXXXXXX Left handed*

# 18

## *The Ravens*

### LILLIE VIOLET RAVEN—HER EARLY LIFE

Lillie Violet Raven was born in Ballards Buildings, Watford in November 1896. The second daughter of Moses and Ada, she seems to have always been the natural leader of her brother and sisters. She held very strong opinions, a fact about which she was quite happy to tell everyone.

Lillie went to school in Watford, near to the High Street, which at that time was an attractive street lined with elm and lime trees. There was also a fountain, and a pond, which I believe is still there. In those days the market was full of meat and produce stalls, with hot chestnut sellers and it was lit by paraffin lamps. Lillie also attended the Watford Town Christian Mission in Farthing Lane, where she was presented with a Marked Testament in February 1906.

When she was fourteen Lillie lived in Cardiff Road, Watford and started work in a chocolate factory, She told us tales of how in those days the workers would clean the utensils by licking off all the chocolate off. She was quite well built even though only five feet two inches tall and became very heavy in later life so I wonder how much of that was due to the amount of chocolate she had consumed as a teenager.

The chocolate factory was called Dr Tibbles Vi-Cocoa factory in Callowland, North Watford. It had opened before 1900 but early in the new century it moved to Windsor Road, North Watford and it was here that Lillie worked. In Watford Museum, there is an advertisement for 'Little Miss Vi's Big Cup Vi-Cocoa', Delectaland, Watford, which is dated around 1907.

Lillie aged 15 at the chocolate factory
Centre back with a spot on her apron

During 1915 Moses Raven and his younger children all moved to London. Ada Hamerdine the oldest daughter was already married to George Harding and had a daughter Alice, Moses' first grandchild. She was the only Raven from this branch of our family to stay in Watford and eventually had seven children. Ada Hamerdine's youngest daughter June, who was born in 1934, has helped with some of our family tree information.

When Lillie got to London she went into service as a housemaid to the playwright Leon M Lion, who had written 'The Chinese Puzzle', which was performed at the New Theatre in 1918. She met quite a few famous artists and writers of the day at his house and may even have answered the door to John Galsworthy, who was a friend of Leon M Lion. Unfortunately the job did not last very long as she fell out with the housekeeper, a German Jewess, who appears to have had even stronger opinions than she did.

Lillie's next job was in a printing factory and at first this went very well. Lillie was always a hard worker and she became a paper pattern folder and kept this job until after she was married. Within a few years, she became the union representative or 'father of the chapel' as it was called in those days. It seems that she was such a militant that the workers in the factory all went on strike, which was most unfortunate for Lillie as the union's in the 1920's did not have the power they do now, so she got the sack for being the "red". Lillie then got a job in a cigarette factory in Euston Road, and considering she spent the rest of her life smoking heavily, she probably enjoyed the perks of this job.

I am sure that had she been a bit older she would have joined the Women's Movement and may have even become one of the militant suffragettes. Her political views never changed throughout her life as she always strongly supported the Labour Party and never missed using her vote.

Charles George and Lillie met shortly after she had first moved to St Pancras and long before he went into the army. It appears that from the first time that they met neither of them ever had eyes for anyone else. They were a prudent couple and decided to save up to get married. Unfortunately, Charles George had to go away to war and he and Lillie sent each other many loving letters and postcards during his army service. Their loving relationship stood both the test of separation and the serious injuries of Charles George and I will continue the story of their marriage in the next chapter.

# 19

## *Wynns and Ravens*

## CHARLES GEORGE AND LILLIE—THE YEARS TOGETHER

On 24th July 1923 the following letter was circulated around the works and offices of Hovenden and Sons:

*August 4th 1923—In view of the approaching marriage of Mr C Wynn the undersigned are desirous of presenting him the usual token and all best wishes for his future happiness.*

A total of six pounds seven shillings and sixpence was collected.—a considerable sum of money in those days.

Charles George and Lillie were married at St Marys, Somers Town, which is just a short walk from Bridgeway Street, where Charles George had gone home to live with his parents after returning from his war service. Charles and Lillie were engaged for a long time as they had decided to save hard and get everything for their home before they married. Lillie always claimed "I had everything down to the last teaspoon in my bottom drawer".

They made their first home in a flat at 73 Victoria Road Camden Town, this has now been renamed Castlehaven Road and the house they lived in is still standing. Lillie was fortunate, as she never had to go out to work during her marriage. The following May she gave birth to her first son Charles Arthur, who she named after her husband, father-in-law and her younger brother. The family lived very simply but comfortably, and four years later their second son William Leslie, named after his uncle and because Lillie liked the name Leslie, was born. This completed their family and the two boys grew up with their large family of cousins. They lived in the same house as their cousins the Collins, and the Embleton cousins also lived nearby in St Pancras.

Charles George and Lillie on their engagement

Every day Charles George went to his work in Berners Street and Lillie took care of their home. They both took great pride in their sons and encouraged them to educate themselves by always attending school, joining the scouts and going to church activities. William Leslie, who at this time was known as Willie, was such a small boy for his age that his father, who was also very small, used to stand above him and say "Are you standing in a hole or am I on horseback".

All of the extended family used to like a drink and they often went to the pub together, but none of them drank heavily as there was not a lot of money to spend in those days. My father told me that the Embleton's and Collins's often used to borrow money from Charles George, as he was the only one in the family who always had a steady income.

Charles George went out regularly to his old comrades club and kept in touch with a few of the men he had served with during his military service, as well as attending the 'The Queens' Royal Regiment Annual Re-union Dinners each year. He made a small donation for some Colours for his former regiment and his name was recorded in the regimental room at Queens House, Croydon. The house no longer exists and the records are now held at the regimental museum at Clandon Park, near Guildford in Surrey,

In 1937 he attended a meeting of many ex-servicemen that had been organised with King George VI in attendance and he was given the following certificate signed by the King.

*I am pleased to see so many old comrades here today.*

*I appreciate your having come, both men and women, in such large number, many of you from long distances, and I hope that you will take lasting memories of this great gathering.*

*I am happy to think that, as Patron, I am in the future to be associated with the work of some of those Bodies, which make up the great Brotherhood of Ex-Service Men. Being one of the Brotherhood myself, I have always followed their progress with real interest and sympathy. I have especially welcomed the interchange of visits between the Ex-Service Men of other countries and ourselves. Those of us who have seen War know what a great calamity it is for victors and vanquished alike, and if, with the united weight of our experience, we can convince the world of this fact then I feel we can render no greater service to the human race.*

*Some among you have not known the tragedy of War, and, I pray God, never will. For you, too there is a task to perform. It is not only in times of common danger that we need the fellow feeling so lavishly outpoured during those dark years. The spirit of unselfishness and sympathy is just as necessary now for the welfare of mankind in our daily life and it is up to you, and to all of us, to see that this spirit is never allowed to fade. These are not easy tasks, but we must all do our best to carry them out: and by setting this example to our fellow-men we shall win honour and glory for the proud name of Ex-Service Man.*

*The Queen and I wish every one of you prosperity and happiness. For us this gathering will always remain one of the outstanding events of our coronation year.*

*George RI*
*27ᵗʰ June 1937*

Charles George loved to play cards, especially cribbage, and he was a member of the St Pancras Reform Club where he played in the winning cribbage team for the Tozer Cup in 1939.

The Wynn family had an above average lifestyle for the times and most years, particularly when their boys were children, they went on holiday. They often travelled to Whitstable, a small town on the Kent Coast at the mouth of the Thames Estuary, but also stayed in Tankerton and Margate in Kent. In the twenties and thirties this was an unusual thing for a working class family to do. Charles George and Lillie often went with Lillie's sister Doris her husband Charles Cullum and their two daughters, Joan and Pat, who were a bit younger than Charlie and Willie. In 1934 we have a picture of them enjoying a holiday at Jaywick in Essex with Lillie's sister Doris and her family. As a result the four cousins grew up together and became very close.

The Wynns and Sheldricks at Whitstable in 1930

On other occasions they also went with one of their Sheldrick step-cousins, Sarah, her husband George Love and their daughter Rosina. On these holidays, they always took 'Nan', the old lady Emma, who was George Sheldrick's widow.

Near the beach at Whitstable was a chocolate machine and young Charlie, as Charles Arthur was always called used to stand in front of this and say "I want something nice", so I am sure he got something nice occasionally.

Hadley Street Jubilee party—1937

The family moved in the early 1930's to 41 Hadley Street, which is near Camden Lock and is now quite an up-market area. At that time it consisted mainly of houses divided into flats, and the one they lived in had their Collins cousins living upstairs. In those day families often shared some of the conveniences that we take for granted today. For the Kings Jubilee in 1937 the whole family met in Hadley Street where they had a street party with the rest of the residents.

The two boys often played with their pretty cousin Maggie Collins and although they were not supposed to play by the lock, as another cousin Alfie Embleton had drowned there in 1931, they played there anyway.

In 1940, Hadley Street and many other parts of St Pancras was bombed, so the extended family of Wynn's, Embleton's, Collins, and Slingsby's were all re-housed but unfortunately not in the same area.

After their home was bombed, Charles George and Lillie moved to Edgware in Middlesex and from then on Charles George had to travel daily on the Northern Line from Burnt Oak to Goodge Street to go to work. Lillie's two sisters, Edith and Doris, also moved to Edgware and Edith's granddaughter, Karen, who took care of her grandmother when she was old, still lives in the same house. The Embleton's and Collins were moved to the Enfield area, which is in North Middlesex and the Slingsby's were relocated to Dagenham in Essex so only Annie and her son William were left in Somers Town and this became the meeting point for all the family.

After he left school Charlie worked as an engineer's fitter for a company called Tanners, and then joined the Royal Navy during the War. Willie was evacuated to Cholsey in Berkshire in September 1939 to stay with Bill and Clara Patey, who were a lovely family and made Willie feel very welcome. They had two children of their own, George, who was eleven and the same age as Willie, and a daughter June.

On Willie's first day when Clara Patey asked him his name and he told her it was William, "That's a pity" she said, "we already have a William here-my husband. What is your second name?" When she was told it was Leslie, she decided that the family would call him Les while he was with them. Shortly after this experience he had a visit from his parents and brother and when Charlie heard the Pateys call him Les he decided that he liked that name better and would call him Les in future. The rest of the family agreed and he has been Les ever since, so I will call him Les for the rest of this history.

Charles George was not fit enough to go to war for a second time and he and Lillie stayed together in St Pancras and then in Edgware. Although there could not have been very much demand for foreign perfumes during the Second World War, Charles George seemed to be popular and secure in his job.

Les who had been evacuated from Hadley Street, returned to his parent's new home in Edgware in December 1941, Edgware was not considered such a dangerous place for a child as St Pancras. During the two years that Les was evacuated the Wynns and Pateys became firm friends and are still in contact to this day.

Charles George did not live to see the end of the Second World War as he died very suddenly in 1944. He had never completely recovered his good health after the Great War and had also suffered from stomach ulcers for many years. One day he had quite a bit of discomfort but had never been one to make a fuss. At Lillie's insistence, he visited the doctor who immediately sent him to Redhill Hospital, which is now Edgware General Hospital. He walked to the hospital where he was admitted straight away, but he never walked away from it, dying there on the 3rd March, less than a week later. His son Charlie, who was stationed in the Navy at Machrihanish, on the Mull of Kintyre in Scotland, was contacted and only managed to get back to Edgware just before he died.

The whole family was devastated.

This letter was sent to his wife Lillie by the Manager of Hovendens.

*29th February 1944*
*Dear Mrs Wynn*
*Please excuse me not writing before as I have had rather a busy time. I thought I would write to you to offer my sincere sympathy in your trouble. I wouldn't worry Mr Wynn with letters especially in the state he is in. When you see him again give him my kind regards and tell him not to worry everything is going OK. I hope he will soon recover. I miss him very much these times. I will try to get down to see him as soon as I can, trusting you will soon have him back again with you and fully recovered.*

*Yours sincerely*
*W Evans*

# OBITUARY
# PUBLISHED IN "THE HAIRDRESSER AND BEAUTY TRADE"
## Death of C. G. Wynn

*We learn with regret of the death, last Friday, after a short illness of Charles George Wynn of 63 Deansbrook Road, Burnt Oak Edgware Mr Wynn was an old and highly esteemed member of the staff of T Hovenden and Sons Ltd and a well known figure to all who visited the Foreign Perfumery Department of their Berners Street Showrooms.*

*He joined the firm in 1912 and except for a three year service with the colours during the last war, when he was wounded, remained with Hovendens ever since.*

*Mr Wynn's friendly personality and unfailing courtesy at all times will be remembered by all who knew him and his untimely passing will be felt and mourned by his associates and friends everywhere. Mr Wynn who was 47 leaves a widow and two sons to whom we offer our sympathy in their great loss.*

# 20

## *Wynns and Ravens*

### LILLIE—THE WIDOW

Although Charles George left Lillie a considerable inheritance for the times, he had never made a will so it took some time to sort it out. On the 14$^{th}$ June 1944 Lillie received 549 pounds 12 shillings and 7 pence, estate duty of 10 pounds 9 shillings and 11 pence had already been deducted. He also had an insurance of 26 pounds from the Liverpool Victoria Friendly Society. Charles George had always been a very thrifty person and regularly bought savings certificates eventually having 456 when he died, a list of which he kept in his diary. Throughout their married life Lillie had never known how much he earned or what he saved. She occasionally used to ask him how much he earned and always got the same answer, "I earn a thousand pounds a year but what I get is another matter".

Lillie was to live for longer as a widow than she had as a wife, but she never stopped loving or missing her husband. Soon after Charles George died, she went to work as a cook in John's Café in Whitchurch Lane in Edgware. A friend that she had previously met in The Boot, a pub in Edgware where she and Charles George had often gone together before he died, needed someone to cook in her café until her son returned from his war service, so Lillie took this on. Her son Charlie was stationed in Australia shortly after his father's death and did not return until 1946. Les started work as an office boy at Imperial Chemical Industries in Mill Hill.

Lillie was a very strong-minded woman and tried to rule her family and her sisters. She was a straight talker, well respected by her neighbours and she loved her two sons. They both knew how to deal with her gently, as beneath this outwardly harsh exterior was a very kind and loving woman. Both sons had a way of living their lives exactly as they wanted, without upsetting her too often.

She settled down to work after the war ended first at Rowlett's, an electrical manufacturer in South Road, Edgware, and then at the Rawlplugs Factory in

Mill Hill. Both Edith and Doris, her sisters, worked on the production line with her and although she left Rawplugs for a short time and went to work in a sweet factory, she eventually returned there working full time until she was seventy-two, when she decided to retire. You could imagine the three Raven sisters, all middle-aged, all with very loud voices, sitting at the production line, chain smoking but all working very hard indeed.

In 1946, Charlie returned from Australia by ship and on board he met a Hong Kong Chinese man who he invited to stay at his mother's house. No one in the family could remember his name as he stayed only a short while, but not long afterwards his businessman brother, who the whole family called Whisky, arrived from Hong Kong also in need of accommodation. He stayed for several years until he married a German girl called Kitty and then moved to Germany with her.

The same year that Charlie returned home he married Kathleen Stack and the young couple lived with Lillie for a short time until they had a home of their own. During this time I was born, Lillie's first grandchild. The Wynn family still met regularly and Lillie would often visit her mother-in-law in St Georges Flats, but inevitably she saw more of her two sisters who had both been re-housed to Edgware and were working in the same factory. Throughout my childhood, I remember them sitting around our dining room table every Saturday night, playing cards, usually Newmarket, and all chain smoking. The Raven sisters all had very loud voices and seemed to compete with one another as to who could speak the loudest, but there was a real affection between them. Whenever they spent the evening with us, the room would be filled with cigarette smoke and it must have been a real health hazard.

Lillie was the first one in the family to have a television and it had such a small screen that she had an enormous magnifying glass over it. Our young cousins were all quite jealous that our Nan had the telly. By this time she had two grand-daughters, my sister Janice and I, and was quite a strict but very kind grandmother. She did not believe in wasting money on silly toys or cheap sweets, but would always give us some of her nice sweets and buy us lovely birthday and Christmas presents.

After Charlie married, Les who had joined the Navy in 1946 as an Ordinary Signalman Tele-printers, finished his service and came home to live with her. Les never married, although at one time he was engaged to a lovely girl called Mary and often had lady friends, so Lillie was very lucky as he eventually took care of her for the rest of her life.

Lillie was a very social person and made the most of her widowhood. Apart from the time she spent with her sisters and the Wynn family, she went to the pub on some evenings after work. On a Tuesday evening she would visit Charlie and Kathy, who had moved to a house just across the road from her, and they went to a great deal of trouble to make her freshly percolated coffee, always with some salt added, just the way she liked it.

Les soon bought his first car, a Hillman, and although all the family seemed to spend hours pushing it up and down the road to get it started, it was the beginning of a new way of life for Lillie. She soon managed to get around to visiting the Embleton's in Enfield and her sister Ada Hamerdine in Watford and also liked to be driven up to Camden Town to see her brother-in-law William Alfred. By this time she was very heavy and weighed about fourteen stone and although she suffered with very bad varicose ulcers on her legs, she did not have any real illness.

Lillie had a green parrot, called Polly of course, that always sat in a cage in the window of her front room. She was very fond of the parrot, which was quite a vicious thing, so her granddaughters always stayed well clear of it. Its shrieking could be heard from the other side of the car park and lawns that were outside her home and even across the main road, but when it died Lillie was very upset.

Lillie with Charlie and Les in 1968

After she retired in 1968, she was still very active and enjoyed life in the same way, even though during the last few years she could not go out without assistance.

The four Raven sisters in 1983
Back Row: Ada Hamerdine & Doris Daisy
Front Row: Edith and Lillie Violet

In 1983 there was a big celebration in Watford to celebrate her sister Ada Hamerdine's 88th birthday, when all four sisters were together for probably the last time. Lillie was 86, Edith 83, and Doris just 75, although unfortunately their brother Arthur had died of cancer in 1964. There was an article in the local paper, The Watford Observer, showing the four Raven girls from Watford, whose ages now totalled 332 years.

One of Lillie's big treats was to have stewed eels on a Saturday. She always cooked them herself and for the fishmonger in Watling Avenue, Burnt Oak it was a regular order. Les normally went shopping for her, but on one particular Saturday he was not around so her daughter-in-law Kathy had to get the eels. These eels were a source of great amusement to my sister and me, as they were swimming around in a metal tin and the customer could pick the one they wanted. Of course well brought up little girls like us would not dream of putting our fingers in the tin to torment the eels especially as they have teeth, or was that our imagination running riot.

Kathy chose the eel she wanted but did not realise that it needed to be killed before she took it home. The fishmonger wrapped it up in a tight parcel and Kathy put it in her shopping trolley. She had not walked more than a few yards down the road when the eel escaped and went straight down a drain, never to be seen again. Kathy would not face her mother-in-law without the eel so, when we had stopped laughing, she went straight back to the fishmonger and bought another one, which she asked the fishmonger to chop up and which she managed to get home safely. I am not sure whether she ever told her mother-in-law or Les what had happened.

The eels were chopped into pieces and cooked in a thick parsley sauce, which was always slightly green in colour. I am remembering this through a child's eyes, as Janice and I spent a lot of time giggling and pretending to throw up while they were being cooked. Eventually they arrived on the lunch table in a big glass bowl and no one but Lillie ate them. She relished every mouthful, having taken her false teeth out before the start of the meal. She would suck the eel flesh from the bones and leave these all around the edge of her plate, which of course brought on another fit of giggles and pretend pukes from her two granddaughters. She was a good sport and took all this teasing without getting annoyed, although we both knew when to stop tormenting her. I have never eaten an eel in my life and have an aversion to them to this day.

Lillie was still regularly going to the White Hart Pub, with Les, and it was only in her last few months that she became confused and did not go out much. She had always called all of her close family by the wrong names, reeling off a list of all her close relatives before eventually getting to the person's correct name.

One morning in January 1985 she did not wake up, she had died peacefully in her sleep in her 90th year.

# 21

## *The Groschs*

### ARTHUR HENRY GROSCH AND ANNIE LEEMING

Arthur Henry Grosch was born on 13 January 1887 in Gloucester Road, St Pancras. He was born into a relatively well-off family, the fifth of six children. Unfortunately his father died when he was only four years old and his mother was left to bring up the children alone.

Little is known about Arthur Henry's childhood, but he does not appear to have excelled at school or to have followed his father's trade as an oil and colourman. After being raised in Harlesden, he moved away from his mother to Castle Road in Kentish Town, where he worked as a Grocer's Assistant. It was here that he met Annie Norah Foley, a young widow, the daughter of William Leeming, who gave his occupation as a bottle washer. Arthur Henry and Annie were married at St Pancras Register office in July 1912 and their first son Frederick was born the following year.

Arthur Henry joined the Northamptonshire Regiment in 1915, but he did not appear to go on active service abroad and was discharged at the end of 1917 for reasons unknown to us. He kept up a correspondence with the army for several months, sending quite a few threatening letters, as it seems that his discharge papers were not sent to him. This meant he could not get a civilian job, so his family must have suffered with no wages coming into the house. During this time he was living at 52 Islip Street Kentish Town.

Once he received his army discharge papers, he became a hospital porter, and he and Annie had six more children, Rose, John James, Winifred and Stanley, their last child, who was born in 1924, as well as twins who died when they were one month old.

When Stanley was still a baby, Annie, who was only 39 at the time, died at what is now Whittington Hospital in Highgate of bronchopneumonia in October 1925. We can only hope she was unaware of her husband's dalliance with another woman and the fact that this lady had given birth to a daughter in the previous May.

We do not know whether Arthur Henry and Annie were still living together, but it certainly looks as if he abandoned their children when she died. Frederick who was twelve, went to live with his grandmother, Eliza, in Bathurst Gardens, Kensal Rise and Rose and John James were fostered out until they were eleven and ten respectively, when they were then sent to a National Children's Home in Harpenden Hertfordshire. These two children lost touch with the rest of their family for many years although they always stayed in contact with each other for the rest of their lives. Both of the two youngest children had a better future, as Winifred was taken and brought up by Annie's twin sisters, and the baby Stanley was adopted by Arthur Henry's younger brother Frederick and his wife Rosetta, who had one son, Frederick, who was born in 1913.

Arthur Henry seems to have given up all responsibility for his children at the time of his affair and marriage to Margaret Stack, but when Rose and John James were fourteen and thirteen, he took them away from the orphanage to live with him again. John James did not get on well with his stepmother and left home as soon as he could to work in a hotel in London, Rose continued to live with her father until she was married.

Arthur Henry Grosch with his daughter Rose in 1942

John James, who is the only one of Arthur Henry's children from his first marriage to whom I have spoken, gave me all this information about his brothers and sisters and said that Frederick, Winifred and Stanley never saw their father again when the family was split up after their mother died.

John James only saw his father twice again after he left the home of his stepmother. The first occasion was when Arthur Henry visited him just after John James was married and he asked him to lend him two pounds, but John James did not have the money so he was not able to do this. When Arthur Henry was taken ill, John James visited him in hospital just before he died of lung cancer on Easter Monday in 1956.

# 22

## *The Stacks*

## MARGARET STACK—THE EARLY YEARS

Everyone who knew my grandmother Margaret had a different opinion of her, ranging from sweet and gentle to barking mad, and she was certainly all of these things and more. Margaret was born in Quinn Buildings, Islington on 1$^{st}$ December 1894 but, for reasons known only to her, always celebrated her birthday on the 4$^{th}$ November. We know very little about her early life apart from the fact that she was certainly quite well educated as she could play the piano well.

Margaret was nineteen when her mother died and the family was living with her oldest brother Walter Cornelius at the time. Her youngest brother Samuel was only fourteen so she had to take on the added responsibility of bringing him up. She worked as a chemical packer and later moved to Hargrave Place in St Pancras. Margaret was a small attractive woman, with a real sense of style and she was definitely the wild one of the Stack family.

She spent all of her life telling us little 'anecdotes' about herself, and although she never actually sat and discussed her early life with anyone she would throw a one liner into a conversation and leave us wondering just what that was all about. No one was ever quite sure which ones were true and which were absolute fantasy, so it could well be that her delusions of grandeur came from information passed on to her by her father about the Stack family in Ireland.

This is the way I have interpreted her life.

Her childhood seemed quite happy although the family was always moving house. She loved all her brothers, but had a special place in her heart for Sammy who had died long before I was born. She never spoke much about her parents so I cannot really judge her feelings for them, but they died when she was a teenager so she missed knowing them as an adult.

She does not seem to have had many men friends when she was growing up but at some time in 1918, when she was twenty-four, she met a 'gentleman farmer from Sussex' who was the son of 'Lady Page'. This was a great romance and Margaret, who was swept off her feet, had hoped they would marry but inevitably they did not. When the romance ended, she never spoke his name again. Of course it had ended because Margaret was pregnant and in September 1919 Margaret gave birth to her only son, Walter Samuel, at 4 Kings Road St Pancras, naming him after two of her brothers. She adored her baby son from the moment he was born and she wanted the best of everything for him, without a doubt he was always her favourite for the rest of her life.

Margaret lost her job when it became apparent that she was pregnant, and as she could not go out to work and bring up her son, she became a laundress and managed to keep herself and Walter Samuel in relative comfort. Her brother Charles, returned from his war service in 1919 and her oldest brother, Walter Cornelius, who had lost his leg in the conflict also came to live with her when he was discharged from hospital. They all lived together with her in Hargrave Place, Holloway, where she was little more than a servant to her brothers. They were to remain a family unit with Margaret caring for them, for the rest of their lives.

Walter Samuel grew up to be a very similar character to his mother. He went to school in Brecknock Road, Holloway and then joined the army serving in North Africa in World War 2. He was engaged to a girl when he went off to fight for his country, but she was run over by a tram in Islington. What a way to die—apparently her bicycle wheel got caught in the tramlines and despite her frantic attempts to free it, the tram ran her over as she attempted to get off her bike. After this Walter Samuel never appeared to take any interest in women whatsoever.

Walter Samuel Stack in 1946

While he was in Egypt, he was badly beaten up and tortured by an Arab gang in the Cairo Souk. Family rumour has it that he was dealing in black market goods but this cannot be proved. He sustained two broken legs and other painful injuries that could not be spoken about, which caused him to suffer a complete mental breakdown and may well have been the reason for his lack of interest in women. He was taken to South Africa where he was hospitalised until he was well enough to be transported home to a mental hospital in Wales. He eventually made a full recovery and came home to live with his mother.

# 23

## *The Groschs and Stacks*

## THE SHORT MARRIAGE

We don't know when Margaret met Arthur Henry Grosch, but by October 1924, a year before his wife died, she was expecting his child. She certainly had not learned anything by her earlier mistake. On the 30th May 1926 her daughter Kathleen was born, at 4 Kings Road, St Pancras. Margaret was so desperate that she decided to let her younger sister Mary Offord, and her husband Charles adopt the baby. Mary would be able to give Kathleen a much more stable upbringing, and Kathleen was given the name Kathleen Offord Stack when her birth was registered, but it was not to be as Margaret could not part with her. This created quite a lot of bad feeling at the time and although the sisters fell out for a while, Kathleen stayed with her mother.

When Arthur Henry Grosch married Margaret Stack at St Pancras Register office on 21st April 1926, he was already living with her in Hargrave Place. The marriage was short lived and knowing Margaret it was probably very stormy. It would have been very hard for any man to live with the Stack family, as they were such a difficult and disparate lot. There was Walter Cornelius, who always considered himself the head of the family, with his one leg and curly nail stomping around on his crutches; Charles who seldom spoke unless he was spoken to; Margaret whose temperament was constantly and completely unpredictable; her six year old son Walter Samuel who was just like her; and the baby Kathleen. With them all living in close proximity to each other in the cottage in Hargrave Place, it was a small wonder that the marriage lasted as long as it did.

Margaret always told everyone who would listen that she threw Arthur Henry Grosch out of the house when her daughter was eighteen months old, which was nine months after their wedding. She claimed that she then obtained a judicial separation but she would never discuss the reasons for this. From that time on she never had anything to do with the opposite sex, and as I grew up would often tell me that men and what they got up to, disgusted her. I suspect she also tried to indoctrinate her daughter Kathleen with this attitude to the opposite sex whilst she was growing up.

Arthur Henry never officially adopted his daughter Kathleen, and she never took his name, remaining Kathleen Offord Stack until her marriage.

What of Arthur Henry, did he go or was he pushed, was he a serial adulterer? Did he and Margaret deserve one another? We know he had a third relationship but we do not know when this started but in 1934, he took two of his children, John James and Rose, out of the orphanage to live with him and his third partner in Vancouver Road, Burnt Oak. John James has told me that both children called this lady Auntie. She was a big woman, but he disliked her so much that he cannot bring himself to remember her name. She bullied him quite badly, made him do a lot of the housework and would not allow him any freedom, even counting the minutes that it took him to get home from school. John James disliked her so intensely, that as soon as he was old enough, he got a job where accommodation was included, in a hotel in central London and left his father's home forever.

Arthur Henry had obviously kept in touch with his daughter, Kathleen throughout her childhood, but I am not sure how, as there were so many secrets kept in the Stack family. When I was a child, he lived around the corner from us and used to stop and talk to my mother Kathleen whenever they met. He seemed a gentle man, but as I was only a small child, I cannot really be a judge. My mother always told me not to tell my grandmother Margaret that we ever met him, and this was probably the only time in my whole childhood when she encouraged me not to tell the truth.

Arthur Henry died of lung cancer on 7th April 1958 in Edgware General Hospital. His death was registered by A.Grosch, his wife, so he and my grandmother may have divorced at some time. If they did they certainly never told their daughter.

# 24

## *The Groschs*

### MARGARET—HER LATER LIFE

Margaret was just thirty-three years old when she and Arthur Henry Grosch parted. She was still a good-looking young woman, although hard work had already taken its toll on her hands. She apparently never looked at another man again, so we cannot help but wonder just how bad her marriage to Arthur Henry was. In the whole of my life I never heard her mention his name and once she moved away from Hargrave Place to Edgware, she was often known as Mrs Stack, although all her pension books and personal papers still had the name Grosch on them. We do not know the reason she chose to get a judicial separation from Arthur Henry, maybe it was just to stop him from marrying again, and as I have said earlier, there may have been a divorce at a later date, but she never uttered a word about this to any of her family.

Soon after Arthur Henry left her, Margaret got a job working in the vegetable cleaning sheds at Covent Garden Market, this was really hard labour and more often than not done by men. However Margaret had to survive, so she got up at the crack of dawn every morning and went to the cleaning sheds where she would clean the vegetables with her hands in cold running water for many hours every day. At home, her brother Walter Cornelius looked after the baby Kathleen, whom Margaret often called Kitty, but that was all he would do, so Margaret had to come home from work to cook and clean for all the family. This life of absolute drudgery went on for several years and although during this time Kathleen went to school, Walter Cornelius still stayed at home. Charles, Margaret's other brother, worked for a printer at this period and was saving hard to buy his own small printing press. It was around this time that Margaret's hands began to suffer badly and she had the first signs of the arthritis, which was to give her so much pain in later years.

In 1935 the family were lucky enough to be re-housed to Edgware in Middle-sex, which was at that time a brand new suburb of London with green fields all around it. The London County Council had built several housing estates and Margaret was offered a house for her and her children on the Watling Estate. This was to be a turning point in her life and all the family including her brothers moved to the brand new house in Banstock Road.

Margaret Stack in 1946

Once they were in Edgware things became better for Margaret, as she managed to get work cleaning houses and also looking after children while their mothers were at work. Charles brought his printing press and set up a small business, so together with Walter Cornelius's war pension, they had enough money to live on.

Margaret was very happy in her new home and would never stop scrubbing it from top to bottom to keep it spotless. She was a terrible cook, she could not leave anything to cook properly and would keep poking at vegetables, stirring cakes in the oven so that all that she ever got was a tin full of cooked crumbs and she always cremated her meat to kill any germs. Most of the time she would be laughing and singing while she worked.

When her son Walter Samuel was old enough, he joined the army and she was very unhappy while he was away fighting in World War Two. She almost pined for him, and she and Kathleen went straight to Wales to see him in hospital when he arrived back from South Africa.

She was very pleased when Kathleen married Charlie Wynn in 1946; she looked very elegant at the wedding, and was still a very attractive woman for her age. The second greatest delight of her life was to arrive the following year when I was born, when she rushed straight out and bought the most expensive pram she could find. She never stopped adoring her son and her oldest granddaughter until the day she died.

Even though she always loved me, I still got out of her way when she was angry. I used to be naughty at times, because she allowed me to do just what I wanted to. One day when I was about five years old and being cheeky to her, I can remember her quite clearly chasing me all around the garden and calling me "a little mare". I am so glad she did not catch me.

Margaret with Sandra in 1948

She used to dance around her dining table with me in her arms singing the song "I'll be loving you eternally". Walter Samuel found her an inlaid wooden music box, which played that tune, and he gave it to my mother when Margaret died and which I still have as a treasured possession.

Margaret never went shopping, but instead she went 'on errands'. She would rush up and down to the Watling Avenue shopping area almost every day on her errands and there was always something in her bag for her granddaughter. My mother told me that she would always give me a loaf of bread to eat when I was in my pram and I would pick the centre out and eat it on the way home.

In 1951 her second granddaughter Janice was born, but although she was a lovely baby, Margaret only had eyes for her older sister. This really annoyed Kathleen, but she had learned at a very young age to keep quiet with her mother as any opposition always led to a row.

Charlie, her son in law, used to say "she was very generous with the local shop-keepers property", as if ever he made the mistake of saying he needed something, it would nearly always arrive the next day. And he was almost certain she had not paid for it. This was something thing that my parents kept a well-guarded secret when I was a child.

She would often 'pop in' to see us, and she was not always welcome as some-times, depending on her mood, she seemed just to have paid us a visit just to have an argument, which would always upset Kathleen. Once when I was naughty and my father told me off, she shouted at him, calling him a sadist. He was the gen-tlest of men, but in Margaret's opinion, no one was allowed to tell me off. More often than not she would just sit down to have a cup of tea with her daughter, and then suddenly 'pop off to do her errands' as she was always in a hurry.

Margaret always like to buy the best cuts of meat, especially for Walter Sam-uel, but she still ruined these when she cooked them. She would always go into the butchers shop and choose her meat telling him that she did not want any old "cagmag". Having an enquiring mind, I looked the word up and found that it meant 'a tough old goose' I have never heard anyone else use this expression, but I still use it to this day when describing tough meat.

As she got older, her delusions of grandeur became more noticeable. She claimed to be a descendant of "Lady Page", who she had previously named as the mother of her first lover. She told us that the Page family were instrumental in setting up the London Omnibus Company and that the family were involved in transport. At one time I tried to find out about this, but could find nothing. I have since discovered that the family were involved in transport, as her father was a Hansom Cab and Fly Driver.

As a child I never saw Margaret drink alcohol and as I grew up I found out why. If she had a drink she became very aggressive, and one night after drinking a port and lemon in a pub, she actually punched a man on the nose. We are not sure what he had done to offend her, but it would not have taken much, and she was very lucky that he chose not to retaliate or bring charges against her. After that incident, Walter Samuel kept her well away from alcohol and public houses.

Walter Samuel had been working as a lorry driver since the end of the War, and before I started school, he often used to take Margaret and me with him if he was going to Southampton docks, as the trip lasted only one day. We used to drive along singing at the tops of our voices and every time we saw a road sign to Southampton we would all shout "Southampton straight up".

In the early nineteen fifties he decided to go into the Merchant Navy where he got a job as a steward on the P & O Cruise Liner Arcadia. Margaret missed him terribly as he was really her reason for living, although they often used to fight like cat and dog. He continued to work on the ship until he had saved enough money to buy her a house and he used to let me count all his money when he was home on leave. I was probably about seven years old at the time and I can remember lots of the large white five-pound notes, so I thought he was extremely rich.

Both of her brothers died during her time in Edgware and so Margaret moved to a smaller house on the same estate. She was not happy here and fell out with all of her neighbours, but fortunately Walter Samuel now had enough money for them to move. He left the Merchant Navy and got a job at the Vauxhall Car Factory in Luton, Bedfordshire and they purchased their first house in Dunstable, a town nearby.

For the next few years, Walter Samuel, very shrewdly, bought and sold houses, always making a profit and eventually paying off his entire mortgage. He always kept a home for his mother and although they were never kept in the pristine condition she had once kept her first house in Banstock Road, he was to take care of her for the rest of her life.

After they moved away from Edgware, they bought houses in Dunstable, Luton, Leighton Buzzard and Linslade, all these towns being quite near to the factory where Walter Samuel worked. Kathleen missed her mother popping in but they often visited us, although they always turned up unannounced, often with their meal of fish and chips wrapped in newspaper.

In the early seventies, they decided to move to Norfolk to be near Margaret's younger sister Mary, and they bought a home in a lovely village called Weeting. Margaret was happy as she had a very nice bungalow, although it was never very tidy, and it was here that she spent the rest of her life. Walter Samuel got a job, which he really enjoyed, as a driver working for the US Air force Base at Laken-heath in Suffolk and from then on we did not see a lot of them.

Margaret's character never changed, she just became more eccentric as she got older, and I remember her visiting me in Hastings in 1971, when she was seventy-seven. By this time Walter Samuel had both a car and a big Norton motorbike. As it was a nice summer day he rode all the way from Weeting in Norfolk to Hastings on the South Coast of England, a distance of over 100 miles, with Margaret on the back of the motorbike. This in itself was quite something special, just to see a little old lady on the back of a motorbike particularly as she had such bad bunions and arthritis, that she was wearing Sainsbury's Supermarket paper bags on her feet, held on by thick elastic bands that she had been given by her postman. I do wish I had taken a photograph. She was in her lady of the manor mood that day, "the descendant of Lady Page", and when she got off the bike she graciously kissed me hello as if she was wearing a tiara and not a helmet. I am sure the neighbours had a few comments to make about her.

Having been light-fingered all of her life, it came as no surprise to her daughter Kathleen to hear that at the grand old age of eighty-two, her mother had been caught 'red-handed' with a frozen chicken under her coat, when leaving Sainsburys Supermarket in Thetford. The store decided to prosecute, which seemed quite reasonable, as they had kept her in paper bag shoes for several years. She was given a conditional discharge because it was her first offence, and of course the magistrate was completely taken in by this sweet little old lady who had absent-mindedly forgotten to pay for her chicken.

Margaret with Walter Samuel and Kathleen in 1977

In her last few years she was very frail and did not go out much. Her eyes used to light up when I visited her, but as she lived so far away I did not see a lot of her. Walter Samuel continued to care for her but she died of bronchopneumonia in St James Hospital, Kings Lynn in January 1978 and is buried in the corner of St Mary's churchyard in Weeting.

Walter Samuel was never very happy after his mother died and became a bit of a recluse. He eventually moved to a flat in Thetford, and he visited his sister occasionally, and like his mother the visit often ended with an argument. Kathleen used to tell her husband that Walter was his relation not hers. I did not see him again after he moved to Thetford and my father and I only visited his flat to clear it out after he had been found dead in his chair there, but that visit alone is almost a story in itself.

Walter Samuel died in February 1996 and he was buried a week later in Thetford Burial Ground.

When my father heard from the police that Walter Samuel had died, they asked him to come to Thetford Police Station to collect the keys to his flat. They also asked him if he would go to Bury St Edmunds hospital to identify the body, as he had named my father as his next of kin instead of his sister. My mother did not want to go and as I could not let my father travel that distance alone, I drove him up to Norfolk.

We arrived at the police station early in the morning and were taken by police car to the hospital morgue to identify the body, which upset my father quite badly. The policeman then gave us the key to Walter Samuel's flat and as we were leaving the police station, he wished us good luck, which seemed quite a strange thing for him to say at that time.

When we arrived at the flat, we realised just why the policeman had said this to us, as we took one look around and decamped to Sainsburys in Thetford for a cup of coffee and to buy bleach, disinfectant and rubber gloves. I will not enlarge on the state of the flat although it was in a terrible mess, but after a couple of hours of hard work cleaning and sorting through piles of old rubbish, we had found over forty thousand pounds, in cash and bonds and various certificates. We rushed around during the rest of that day organising his funeral and sorting out all of his papers, even managing to arrange with the local council to clear his flat, so that we would never have to return to it again.

We wondered for a long time afterwards how much money we might have thrown away.

# 25

## *The Flynns*

## ALFRED JAMES FLYNN AND EDITH MAY HUGHES

Alfred James Flynn was a handsome man with wonderful blue eyes that were passed on to his grandson Bob and to your father Stuart. He had the most wonderful sense of humour and would always make jokes.

Alfred was born in 1900 at 2 Hopkins Street, Westminster. I know nothing of his childhood until he was 21 when he married Edith May Hughes, the daughter of Arthur Edwin Hughes, a Railway Carman, and his wife, the former Minnie Bailey. The wedding took place in Portsmouth where Alfred was stationed in the Army. We do not know where Alfred and Edith met, but she was living in Southsea at the time of the marriage. The Hughes family came originally from St Pancras and Edith was born in Prince of Wales Crescent, but they all moved to Hastings early in the twentieth century.

Alfred was quite an ambitious man and soon owned his own home in Riverdene, Edgware in Middlesex. The house he brought for £550 in the 1930's is now worth in excess of £500,000 pounds and is considered a very desirable residence.

During the Second World War he served in North Africa and won the British Empire Medal. He and Edith went to Buckingham Palace to receive it from King George VI.

After his Army service, Alfred became a telephone engineer and this was his job until he retired. In the telephone exchanges, he was always very popular and used to throw sweets over the switchboards to the telephonists when the supervisors were not looking.

Alfred always drove a Reliant three wheeled car and used to drive for miles to find the cheapest petrol. In 1970 when he had his first heart attack and had to give up driving, he gave his Reliant to me, I am ashamed to admit that I would not be seen driving it and soon exchanged it for a green mini which both your father and Uncle Andrew will remember. Alfred did not mind this at all as he always seemed to have a soft spot for me. Once he retired, he spent his life working on his garden and was very active until he died of a heart condition in 1973.

Edith seemed to me to be the opposite of her husband but as I only knew them in later life, I cannot really be a judge. She spent a lot of time bringing up her grandson Bob when he was a child and she always loved him very much. In the early nineteen-sixties she developed a brain tumour, but it was successfully operated on, although she was quite deaf for the rest of her life this may have made her a quieter person than she was before the operation.

When her grandson Bob and I became engaged, she would go out once a week and buy us something for our home, such as tea towels, steak knives, dusters, all sorts of essentials and she was always very generous to us throughout our marriage.

At this time Alf and Edith would go to Woolworth's in Burnt Oak every Saturday afternoon to say hello to Janice your great aunt who had a Saturday job there.

Alfred and Edith had two sons, the oldest, Alf, was born in 1921 and the youngest, Paddy, who was about five years younger. We will talk about Alf in the next chapter, as he is your great-grandfather.

Paddy Flynn was a very amiable man and like his father in many ways. He was married to Maureen, who was a gentle woman whom I liked very much, but unfortunately I did not see much of either of them after my marriage as they soon moved to Templepatrick in Northern Ireland because Paddy's work took him there. In the early sixties, they adopted two children, Russell and Karen. Russell and Karen acted as my pageboy and bridesmaid when I married your grandfather. I am not sure if either Paddy or Maureen are still alive.

Edith outlived her husband by many years and sold the house in Riverdene retiring back to a flat in St Leonards on Sea to be near her family. Although her son Alf lived very near to her, she remained independent until the end of her life and she died in St Leonards in 1989.

# PART VI
## The mid 20ᵗʰ Century

◆

*Wynns, Stacks and Flynns*

# 26

## *The Wynns*

### CHARLES ARTHUR WYNN—THE EARLY YEARS

Charles Arthur Wynn, your great grandfather was born at 73 Victoria Road, St Pancras in May 1924, the first son of Charles George and Lillie Violet Wynn. His brother William Leslie was born four years later. Even though he was my father I am very biased about Charles Arthur Wynn because, like most of his predecessors, he was one of the loveliest, gentlest men I have ever met and I loved him dearly.

Charlie, as he was always known, and his younger brother Les had a very happy childhood and they certainly never went without anything. Their parents always loved them both very much and it was a very happy family. Charlie was very lucky to survive when he was a baby as he had whooping cough, which in those days without antibiotics was often fatal. He spent four months in hospital and, luckily for us, made a complete recovery.

Charlie went to Holy Trinity School, Hartland Road, Kentish Town when he was five and stayed there until he transferred to the senior school in Great College Street when he was eleven. When he first went to school his older cousin Kitty Embleton used to take him every day. Charlie enjoyed school where he was a popular boy, and he always took care of his little brother. Although he was intelligent, Charlie never took any examinations while he was at school, preferring to leave at fourteen to become an apprentice engineer.

The two boys had a wonderful childhood, often going out for the day to play on Hampstead Heath. In later life Charlie, who knew the whole of the heath so well, would often bring his own daughters there for walks, with the whole family walking from Golders Hill Park, through the Heath and across Parliament Hill Fields to have tea with their great uncle William Alfred Wynn.

One of Charlie's early memories was of standing at the top of Parliament Hill Fields, watching the Crystal Palace burn down in 1936. It had been moved to Sydenham in South London after the Great Exhibition in Hyde Park closed.

Charles George and Lillie could not do enough for their two boys and encouraged them to join the scouts, so Charlie became a member of the 8th St Pancras Scouts, he always enjoyed scouting and he and Les were regulars in the local Gang Shows put on by their scout troop. Charlie loved going to the scout camp, especially pushing the handcart full of the tents and camping equipment, which in those days was pretty rudimentary, to Mill Hill East where they camped in a field next to the gasworks. Charlie also went on a scout camping trip to Guernsey an island that he always wanted to visit it again, but he never did manage to go back. He often joined a Sunday school, but only for the few weeks before their outings so that he could go to the seaside with them.

When Les was six, he was run over by a car in Prince of Wales Road. He was knocked up in the air and landed flat on his back, then spent ten days recuperating in hospital. The man who had knocked him down, got out of his car, scooped him up in his arms, and took him straight to St Pancras Hospital. Poor Charlie who had seen the accident happen, had to run home to his mum and tell her what had happened, but the problem was, that no one knew where Les was. Eventually they found Les safely in hospital, but fortunately, once he returned home again he appeared to be none the worse for his ordeal. This incident proved too much of a shock for Charlie who was probably supposed to be taking care of him, that he appeared to have had some sort of severe reaction, or maybe even a mild stroke, as he lost the use of the left side of his body and the sight in his left eye was affected. The numbness in his arms and legs wore off over the next few months, but he had to wear glasses for the rest of his life.

Charles George and Lillie had bought a piano for Charlie and Les on which they were regularly given lessons, but after the accident Charlie had to give up the lessons. He probably wasn't too sorry about that, although Les continued with his lessons until he was evacuated to Berkshire when the Second World War broke out.

Charlie in 1925

Charlie always said that Les could get away with murder with his mum so the following conversation would often take place on a Sunday morning when they were in bed with Charlie saying to Les,

"Go and ask Mum for a sweet"

Les—"You ask her"

Charlie—"No, you ask her or I'll tell her what you did"

Les—"What did I do?"

Charlie—"You know what you did"

Les—"I didn't do anything"

Charlie—"Oh yes you did and if you don't ask Mum for a sweet, I'll tell her what you did"

So Les would go and get sweets for them both, never knowing that he really hadn't done anything.

Both boys were given a halfpenny a day pocket money and Les was also given a penny to buy two thirds of a pint of milk at school every day because he was 'small and pale', and the milk was supposed to build him up.

When Charlie left school in 1938 he started work with an engineering company called Tanners where he trained as an Engineer, Fitter and Turner. He stayed in this job until 1942, when he volunteered for military service and went into the Navy at the age of eighteen.

Charles Arthur Wynn FX101465. Air Fitter-Fleet Air Arm. For Charlie, his time in the Navy was the worst time of his life. He went to join up with his best friend Charlie Pereira, and they both wanted to be stokers. Charlie Pereira got his wish, but as Charlie Wynn was an engineer he had to join the Fleet Air Arm.

He hated service life and could not stand what he thought was the petty snobbery that went on between the officers and ordinary seamen. He certainly did not like being spoken down to and wondered sometimes how he managed never to react. Although he always abided by them, he could not stand the many rules that seemed to govern every minute of his day. He never divulged these thoughts to a single person while he was serving and did his work to the best of his ability, but after he was back in Civvy Street he vowed never to have anything more to do with the Navy.

The Navy left its mark on him and for the rest of his life he could never bear opinionated people telling him what to do, unless there was a really good reason for it. He never liked going to expensive restaurants and being served by what he considered servile waiters, which for some reason reminded him of service life.

Charlie Wynn at 18

After he joined the Navy, Charlie was sent to HMS Duke at Warrington for his training. He was then stationed at Burton-on-Trent and then transferred to RAF Machrihanish Campbelltown, which is on the Mull of Kintyre in Scotland, where he worked as an aircraft fitter. It was while he was here, that he got the terrible and unbelievable news that his father was gravely ill and was not expected to survive. He frantically made the journey back to Edgware, just in time to see his beloved father before he died. Many relatives have told me that Charlie and his father were "as alike as two peas in a pod" and certainly the photos show a resemblance.

Not long after his father died, Charlie was posted to Australia and it was here that he spent the rest of the war. He travelled there on the Union Castle. In Australia he served at HMS Nabsford in Brisbane with men from the Air Force and the American and Australian Services. He enjoyed the camaraderie with his fellow engineers and had some good times, including one night when he got locked up in clink for being drunk. No charges were made and he was let out once he was sober. It was in Australia that he was awarded a good conduct medal 1$^{st}$ Class, but he never collected it or the Chevron awarded in 1943.

One the best things that Charlie liked about Australia was the food. There was so much to eat there in comparison with the rationing in wartime Britain, so he particularly liked being on canteen duty. He always hoped he would be able to buy Lamington cakes in England but I don't think he ever did.

While he was in Australia he had a girlfriend named Grace, who came from a strict Baptist family from the Blue Mountains. It was not a serious romance, but he seemed to have some nice memories of her. As his daughters grew up, they used to tease him about 'Amazing Grace' and their alleged half brother and sister 'Bruce and Sheila', who, they joked owned the Wynn's Winery in Coonawarra before they went walkabout. Charlie took it all in with his usual good humour, but the joke did not always go down to well with their mother.

One night in Brisbane when he was late getting back to camp after an evening out, Charlie knew he would be in trouble if he did not get a move on, so he tried to save time by running across a field that was pitch black. Unfortunately for him the field was not empty and he ran straight into a horse's backside, and afterwards he said he did not know who was the most shocked, him or the horse.

Charlie wanted to get home to England as he worried about his widowed mother and he eventually left Australia in 1945 and came home by sea, crossing the line on the Stirling Castle on 9th March and stopping off in Bombay on the way.

Charlie in Bombay in 1946–1ˢᵗ left

When Charlie returned from Australia he went to HMS Daedalus at Lee-on-Solent until he was discharged. This is now the scene of civil unrest as our government is hoping to fill it with Asylum seekers and the local residents do not want them.

After his war service, he immediately went back to his old engineering job at Tanners. He was young, fit and handsome, and about to meet the woman who would mean more than anything else to him for the rest of his life.

# 27

# *The Stacks*

## KATHLEEN OFFORD STACK—THE EARLY YEARS

In comparison with her Charlie, my lovely mum Kathleen did not have an easy childhood, and she was an unhappy little girl a lot of the time. She was born in May 1925, the second illegitimate child of Margaret Stack, and had an older half brother Walter Samuel with whom she grew up. Brother and sister were never very close, particularly as Walter Samuel used to bully her, but she could always rely on her Uncle Walter Cornelius, who was always her protector.

Her father, Arthur Henry Grosch, who was still married to his first wife when she was born, had married her mother Margaret when she was eleven months old, but he had disappeared from the marital home by the time she was eighteen months old. Although she saw him occasionally in later life, he was never to have any influence over her upbringing.

It is a puzzle to all of us how she had remained in touch with her father, as he left her mother when she was too young to have any memory of him. There is no doubt that there would have been hell to pay if her mother had ever found out that Kathleen and her father were in contact with each other.

Margaret always worked very hard to keep Kathleen well dressed and fed, but she always favoured her son. She did not neglect Kathleen physically, but she did not have a lot of time for her little daughter, seldom showing her any love and affection.

Luckily for Kathleen, her two uncles were on hand throughout her childhood and they were the ones who gave her the love and affection she desperately needed, and who really brought her up. It seems rather sad that Kathleen never knew she had five older half brothers and sisters by her father's first marriage, but we only discovered this after she had died.

When Kathleen was five, she started school at Hungerford Road in Upper Holloway and stayed here until she was about ten. We have a picture of her taken at this school in which she looked a very unhappy little girl.

The family then moved to Edgware and it was here that she continued her education at Burnt Oak School in the Edgware Road. Kathleen did not like school at all and having read her diaries, I think she may have been slightly dyslexic, which probably caused a lot of her misery. She always had a very good memory and loved reading books, but she seems to have had a lot of time away from school with various mystery illnesses. This was probably not helped by the fact that her mother did not bother too much whether she went to school or stayed at home.

Kathleen Stack at school in 1935 2nd row 1st right

Kathleen when she first came to Edgware

Kathleen was always a very modest person, who was easily embarrassed, and who could never discuss bodily functions of any kind at any time. Even when we were children we seldom saw her walk around in her underwear and certainly never undressed. She found it impossible to tell either of her daughters the facts of life and when I was about eleven years old, she almost threw a book at me and told me to read it alone. I knew I could ask no questions, but as most children of our time discussed every aspect of sex with each other, it was not a problem. As I grew older I began to wonder what must have happened to her in her childhood to make her so sensitive about such things.

Kathleen Stack in 1945

Kathleen left school at the first possible moment she could and as she had no qualifications, went to work in a factory called Irie Resistors working on the production line. Within a short space of time she changed jobs and went to Chas. Wright and Co in Church Way, Edgware, where she made car number plates. When the war started she joined the Civil Defence Volunteers and became an Air Raid Warden, spending many nights patrolling the streets around her home, and she seems to have enjoyed doing this.

She was an attractive looking young woman who had several romances in her teens, and even became engaged to at least two of her admirers. I think she was trying to escape from her unhappy home life into marriage and it was her good fortune that she did not marry either of her early suitors but waited for Mr Right, who unbeknown to her, was on his way back from Australia.

# 28

## *Wynns and Stacks*

## CHARLIE AND KATHY—OVER FIFTY YEARS TOGETHER

Charlie Wynn and Kathy Stack met at the White Hart Pub in Edgware High Street on her 21st birthday. Kathy was there with a group of her friends having a birthday drink and Charlie, having not long returned from Australia, wandered in to see if any of his pals were around.

For Charlie, it was love at first sight, and he managed to talk her into letting him walk her home. It seems amazing that they had both grown up in St Pancras, then moved to Edgware, only lived a five-minute walk away from each other, but had never met before.

They arranged to meet again the next day and Charlie was knocking on her door early the next morning to take her out. They spent the whole day together and Charlie brought her a handbag as a belated birthday present. They were seldom apart after that and managed, against much opposition, to arrange a fairly big white wedding just three months later.

It was bound to fail—it lasted forever.

Charlie's mother, Lillie, was not too pleased and wanted them to wait a while, in fact she never really wanted either of her sons to ever leave home. However, Charlie and Kathy would not wait, so she put on a brave face and grew to love her daughter-in-law.

They were married at John Keble Church in Mill Hill in September 1946 they had known each other just 100 days.

The wedding was quite a grand affair for one held so soon after the war and no expense was spared. Kathy looked beautiful in her white silk dress and Charlie was wearing his demob suit. Les was Best Man and two of Charlie's cousins were bridesmaids. Even after this distance in time, so long after their wedding, I can

133

sense the influence of Lillie and many food ration coupons were saved to ensure there was a sit-down meal of roast beef at Kathy's new mother-in-law's house.

September 8th 1946
Les, Lillie, Pat Cullum, Charlie & Kathy,
Nancy Walker, Margaret, Walter Samuel

For their honeymoon the couple had a day out in Southend on Sea where Charlie brought Kathy a plastic Golliwog brooch, which she kept for the rest of her life.

The two mother's-in-law, Lillie and Margaret, lived within five minutes walk of one another and, although they never argued or fell out, they both spent the rest of their lives avoiding each other.

In post-war London there was a housing shortage and Charlie and Kathy did not have anywhere to live, so they moved in with his mother who would have been happy for them to stay with her forever. This is not a good idea for any newly married couple and it seems that there were quite a few arguments. Kathy was not her mother's daughter for nothing and the sparks certainly flew in those first few weeks. Things got pretty fraught so they decided to move in with

Kathy's mother, her brother and the two uncle's, but this turned out to be even worse and Charlie, gentle soul that he was, almost ended up fighting with her brother, who still tried to bully his married sister.

By this time there was an added bonus, a baby was on the way so it meant that, if they were lucky, they would probably be able to get a council house. For a short while they both stayed with their respective mothers, but they could not bear to be apart so they chose to go back to the least confrontational of the two mothers. Kathy bit her tongue, and they both moved back in with Lillie, which was definitely the best choice they could have made. A few weeks later, Kathy fell down the stone stairs to Lillie's maisonette and I was born later that day, several weeks early, weighing only about four pounds. Lillie at once announced that I looked like a skinned rabbit. I was baptised at John Keble Church two weeks later and they all had their work cut out for the next few months keeping me alive, but something called M & B's apparently did the trick and I am still here to write this history.

Soon after my arrival, Charlie and Kathy were lucky enough to be offered a house in Fryent Crescent, West Hendon and here they settled down to a very happy life together with their baby daughter. The house was not that convenient if you judge it by today's standards as they had an outside lavatory and no hot water. In the corner of the kitchen was a large copper, which was used to heat water and wash the clothes. Although there was a bathroom upstairs, I can never remember using it, but have lovely memories of the tin bath in the kitchen and of jumping out of it into my mother's arms and having a warm towel wrapped around me.

Charlie was still working as an engineer at Tanners in St Pancras at this time and he used to ride his bike to work each day to save money. It was a long journey and before too long, he decided to find something that was nearer to home. Jobs were not so easy to find and he ended up taking a job as a bus conductor with London Transport until he could find another engineering job. The job was not very well paid and the shift work was terrible, but at least he only had to go to Hendon Bus Garage to start work. He only had one slight mishap throughout the entire time he worked for London Transport, when he lost his bus one day during the 'great smog' of 1953. His driver could not see where he was going and asked Charlie to lead the way. He then got off the bus, which moved away, but he never saw it again. My father told me that the smog was so thick that he could not even see his hand in front of his face, so the only thing he could do was to walk back to the bus garage and wait for his bus to return.

Life was very happy in Fryent Crescent and Kathy and Charlie gradually got their home together. Margaret was a regular visitor because you could not keep her away from her baby granddaughter. They had some pleasant neighbours and I had a little playmate called Christopher Windmill who lived next door.

Kathy took a job at the Schweppes 'you know who' factory in 1950 because I could be taken care of in their nursery. I vaguely remember being given bread and jam to eat and of being made to lie down and sleep when I wanted to play, but I fretted for my mother so she gave up the job after a very short time.

In 1951, the family became complete when Janice Patricia was born at home in Fryent Crescent. She was the first baby in Hendon to have a one-dustbin-lid-salute, as Charlie, when he was given the afterbirth to dispose of, did it only too well. He went into the garden and made a fire in a dustbin, put in the afterbirth, covered it in petrol, set fire to the paper, and put the lid on. As he walked back down the garden there was an almighty bang and he turned around to see the dustbin lid flying high in the sky. What a way to announce a birth, I prefer the Times myself.

I was bought some mice as a present when my little sister was born, but after only a few days they began to smell really bad even though both of my parents kept scrubbing the cage out. I was not terribly interested in the mice so they were soon relegated to the outside lavatory but the smell got so bad that I refused to go in there and used to run around to the house next door and use their toilet instead. I never did know what happened to the mice, but they soon disappeared.

I loved my little sister, and my mother told me I never showed any signs of jealousy when she was born. One day when she was just over a year old, my mother asked me to put her socks on. She was sitting on the bottom stair and would not keep her feet still, so I bit them. Of course my sister made the most awful fuss and I got into serious trouble. My mother made me sit down on the stairs and did the same to me, although I do not think she hurt anything more than my pride. I expect today it would be called child abuse, but it taught me a lesson and I have never bitten anyone since.

Charlie, Kathy Sandra and Janice
at Fryent Crescent in 1952

In the spring of 1952 when my sister was still a baby, my parents took us to Finsbury Park to go on one of the last tram journeys in London. My father thought that it was important for us to take part in, what to him appeared to be the end of an era. I can still remember the ride as it was extremely bumpy and I also recall the shiny brown leather seats that were very slippery. I had to climb up to get onto them and I can still see myself sliding the length of the seat whenever the tram stopped.

Soon after Janice was born, Kathy started to do homework to supplement the family income and she would hand-finish Irish Embroidery on expensive blouses. It was absolute slave labour, as boxes and boxes of these exquisite blouses were delivered and there was always a deadline to be met. The work was quite intricate and Kathy kept it up for quite a long time. Family life was always very happy, but unfortunately with the stress of the homework, Kathy became ill with depression and she did not want to leave the house. The doctors told her that it was mainly the result of her traumatic childhood and she did not recover properly for several years.

Charlie who was always so supportive, loved her dearly and could not bear to see her so unhappy, so he desperately searched for a job that would give him more sociable hours in order that he could spend more time with her and his two little girls. Eventually he found one in Edgware, which suited him, and the factory was in the same road that his mother lived in, so he went to work for Boosey and Hawkes as a musical instrument maker and polisher. This was a very well paid job in comparison with his last one, it was very dirty work but at least he was able to earn enough money so that Kathy no longer had to take in homework.

Although this was a great help, it happened too late for Kathy and she was admitted to hospital suffering from complete nervous breakdown. She was in hospital for just over a week when another female patient threatened her with a knife. The nurses disarmed the woman, but this was enough to make Kathy decide to deal with her problems in her own way and she discharged herself, which was probably the most sensible thing she could have done.

Kathy was to suffer with her nerves for the rest of her life and although most of the time she seemed completely well, she always needed medication until the day she died. She was such a methodical person that I cannot imagine that she ever-missed taking one of her tablets.

It was around this time that I started school at the Hyde School in Hendon and I can remember my mummy being so proud of me when I won the egg and spoon race. I won a china doll, which she immediately took off me so that I would not break it. When we arrived home, she put on the mantelpiece and told everyone who came to the house why it was there. It is now sitting in my house, still on show, although it is one of the ugliest dolls you have ever seen.

By the time I was six years old, my mother would allow me to go up the road to meet my daddy when he came home from Edgware on his bicycle. He would then let me stand on one of the pedals and we would ride the last half a mile home together.

Once Charlie started work in Edgware, they decided to try to move back there so that he could be nearer his job and they would also be nearer both of their mothers. They applied to exchange their council house and in 1954 they were lucky to get an exchange with a house in Littlefield Road, Burnt Oak that was just ten minutes walk from the Boosey and Hawkes factory and very close to both Lillie and Margaret.

Charlie and Kathy Wynn moved to Littlefield Road in Edgware in the spring of 1954 and they could not have been happier, The house itself was in need of some renovation, but at last they had an inside lavatory and a copper with a hand pump so twice a week water could be pumped upstairs to the bathroom and the family could have hot baths.

Outside their home in Littlefield Road, Edgware

In the kitchen Charlie soon had an Ascot gas water heater installed and over the next few years, Kathy got her twin tub washing machine, refrigerator, vacuum cleaner and a water heater in the bathroom. From then on we bathed every single day, which was an absolute luxury at the time. Today you could not imagine living like this but at the time we all considered ourselves very lucky.

Over the next few years the Wynn family routine followed a similar pattern. We would spend Christmas Day at home with Lillie and Les, who always came to dinner, and then Edith, Lillie's sister, would invite us all to go to her Christmas party at her house. On Boxing Day Charlie and Kath would usually invite Margaret and Walter Samuel but they did not always come as it all depended on Margaret's mood on the day. Saturday night was always a cards evening, and they would play Newmarket or Pontoon with Lillie and her sisters, while they chain-smoked and made the whole house smell, This meant that we spent Sunday mornings with all the windows open, even during winter, so no wonder we went to Church.

Every year our parents took us on lovely holidays, sometimes on the Isle of Wight, sometimes in Norfolk. In fact, Charlie and Kathy gave their two daughters a very happy and stable childhood.

At the end of the fifties, Charlie bought his first car, but unfortunately it took him three times to get through his driving test. Although his driving was okay, he completely lost his nerve when taking the test and at the third attempt he went to his doctor to get something to calm him down.

Charlie's first car was a Ford Popular, with the registration number 627 YMK and the family went for many outings in it.

During most of this time Kathy's nerves were stable but her health had deteriorated. She had several major operations, for a stomach ulcer, gall bladder and two operations on the arteries in her arms and one her legs, as they had become blocked. The operations were called symathectomies, which apparently cut sympathetic nerves to stop the pain caused by narrow veins. This serious condition was partly blamed on her taking the high dosage birth control pill, as she was one of the first women to be prescribed the pill. After these operations she had to take more medication to keep her blood thin, so by her mid-forties she was on a daily cocktail of prescription drugs.

In 1967, they took their first foreign holiday to Italy, and Kathy who had never seen her birth certificate, applied for a copy so that she could obtain a passport. She was really upset to find out that she was illegitimate and felt completely humiliated about the whole situation. At the time, she never spoke to her mother about the circumstances of her birth because she could not be sure how badly Margaret would react to any questions, so to mention anything about it then, would not have been a wise thing to do. However poor Kathy felt very embarrassed and none of the family could convince her that it really did not matter.

Picking her moments very carefully, over the next few years, Kathy eventually found out the truth surrounding her birth. It was during this time that she learned that her mother had considered giving her away at birth and this was the reason for her being given the second name of Offord.

Charlie's one claim to fame was a television appearance on the BBC children's programme called Playschool, where he was shown with the musical instruments he made and cleaned. His grandson Andrew was watching the programme one day and could not believe his eyes when he saw his granddad. "That's my granddad, that's my granddad," he shouted.

Charlie and Kathy were able to buy their house, when the government announced a scheme for tenants to buy their council houses. They had enough saved for a deposit and had organised a mortgage. They decided to go to Weeting in Norfolk and visit Kathy's mother and brother to tell them the good news. Walter Samuel immediately told them not to take out the mortgage as he had enough money under his bed to pay for the house in full and he would make them an interest free loan. They then proceeded to count the money, which had never been counted for years but just tucked away as he earned it. Charlie then drove home, from Weeting to Edgware, with a bag full of mixed bank notes, feeling as if he had robbed a bank.

Charlie suddenly decided to leave Boosey and Hawkes in the early seventies as a friend called Charlie Marsh, who he had known at school and had worked with on and off since he was a boy, had a coronary thrombosis and died next to him in the factory. He could not settle down after this and decided that he would find an easier job, with no stress or deadlines, to see him into retirement.

We all suggested that he became a postman and this is what he did. The salary was less than half of what he had earned before, but he was content and despite the fact that he did not like getting up at four in the morning he enjoyed his job. Kathy at this time had a part-time job at the Metropolitan Police training college, so they had their afternoons together.

Charlie took up fishing as a hobby when he moved to Edgware and as well as his early morning trips to the River Thames at Cookham Reach and the lakes by Heathrow airport, he also used to drive to Hastings and go sea fishing. One day he took your grandfather Bob Flynn, who was also a keen fisherman, with him to Cookham where unfortunately Bob became ill and collapsed unconscious into the river. Bob was fully clothed in his winter fisherman's outfit and began sinking fast. He would have drowned if Charlie had not had the presence of mind to realise that he had not just fallen in. Even though he was also fully clothed complete with heavy wader boots, Charlie did not hesitate to jump into the fast running water to save Bob's life. It is only because of his brave action that you are here, as this incident happened several years before your father was born.

What more is there to tell about the Wynn Family? Charlie and Kathy retired to Eastbourne in 1987, where they bought themselves a delightful bungalow with a river in the back garden. Charlie used to feed the swans and ducks but Kathy was not too thrilled if they came into the house when he forgot.

They had eleven happy years in Eastbourne and celebrated their Golden Wedding Anniversary in 1996. Les joined them in Eastbourne, he also bought a bungalow in the same road when he retired five years later, so the family once again had left their roots behind.

Charlie and Kathy loved to be with their two daughters and spent as much time as they could with both of them. They enjoyed watching their three grandsons grow up, but they were always happier with just one another.

With their grandsons in Eastbourne
in September 1986

In January 1998 Kathy was taken ill with breathing problems. She was diagnosed as suffering from lung cancer and five weeks later she died with her Charlie at her side.

Charlie got on with his life as best he could and even managed to break his ankle jumping off a narrow boat on his 76th birthday. He spent as much time as he could with both of his daughters but he missed Kathy dreadfully and he did not want to be with us any longer. Two years after her death he collapsed and died of a brain haemorrhage. I think he died of a broken heart.

Not a day goes by when I don't miss them.

When Janice and I we were in his house on the morning he died we found the following poem that he had written out and left for us underneath the calendar he changed the date on every day.

*Remember me when I am gone away,*
*Gone far away into the silent land;*
*When you can no more hold me by the hand,*
*Nor I half turn to go*
*Yet turning stay.*
*Remember me when no more day by day*
*You tell me of our future that you planned:*
*Only remember me;*
*you understand*
*It will be late to counsel then or pray.*
*Yet if you should forget me for a while*
*And afterwards remember,*
*Do not grieve:*
*For if the darkness and corruption leave*
*A vestige of the thoughts that once I had,*
*Better by far you should forget and smile*
*Than that you should remember and be sad.*

Christina Rossetti

# 29

## *The Flynns*

### ALFRED JAMES FLYNN AND ELSIE MAY CROSS

Your great grandparents, Alf and Elsie were a happy couple who cared about each other deeply but did not like to publicly show any affection. They were both very hard workers and spent a lot of time improving their homes, with Alf doing most of the work, and not employing tradesmen, as he could turn his hand to almost anything.

Elsie always kept their home in a spotless condition, and I know that, whenever they invited me to tea, she used to get the vacuum cleaner out after I left. Elsie could never hide her thoughts and whatever she thought of you was written all over her face. I am afraid that on many occasions I did not come up to her expectations as a daughter-in-law and in the end she was certain these feelings were justified.

I was still quite fond of them when I was married to your grandfather and in the early days of our marriage both Alf and Elsie did a lot to help us. This especially applied to Alf, who changed our boiler and helped with the decorating when we did not know what to do.

Alf was born in Alfred Street, St Leonards in 1921 and as far as I know, there are still members of the Hughes family living there. He spent some of his childhood away from home on a farm and then went into the army.

I do not know where Alf and Elsie met but it could have been while they were both in the services. They married on Christmas Eve 1942 in Hendon Register Office, North West London. Alf was a Gunner with the Middlesex Regiment and Elsie was in the Women's Auxiliary Air Force.

Elsie was born in September 1942 in Medrose, St Teath Camelford, Cornwall, and her parents were John Cross, who was a farm labourer, and Elizabeth Jane Fanson. Both of her parents had been married before but their spouses had died. John came from Camelford and Elizabeth from Morwinstow in Cornwall.

Elsie did have at least one brother that I had heard about but I know no more about her family, as she did not keep in close contact with them. I have traced her family back a little further but do not have much information on them so this is little more than a list.

The parents of John Cross were John Henry Cross, a slate quarryman, who was born in 1847 in Okehampton, Devon and Susannah Hora, who was born 1851 at St Endellion, Cornwall

The parents of Elizabeth Jane Fanson were John Thomas Fanson, a farm labourer, and Elizabeth Darch.

The parents of Susannah Hora were John Hora, a farm labourer, and Susannah Amey.

Alf was in the Army throughout the war and Elsie left the Women's Auxiliary Air Force to have their only child, Robert James, in 1944. She soon went back to work leaving her son with her mother-in-law and became a wages clerk, eventually working in the same factory, Rawlplugs, as my grandmother and great aunts. It was there that a robber once held her up by putting a gun to her head when he stole all the week's wages for the factory. She never got over it and was happy a few years later to leave the job to run her own business with her husband.

Elsie had a double mastectomy when she was in her early thirties and this definitely caused her a great deal of misery throughout her life.

Alf, in the meantime, became a telephone engineer, working his way up to a senior position before he took early retirement. He and Elsie were able to buy a Village Stores in St Mary's Bay, Kent and they turned it into a successful mini-supermarket before selling this business to buy another small shop in Hastings.

The second shop in Beaconsfield Road, Hastings was very close to where your grandfather and I were living at the time, and this is where Alf and Elsie stayed until their retirement.

At this time, your grandfather and I were divorced and he went back to live with them. Your grandfather had been ill since he was about twenty years old, with an inoperable brain tumour and although it made him have seizures and affected his behaviour, the doctors told us it was not life threatening. When Alf and Elsie sold their business, they all moved to back to St Leonards where, within a year, your grandfather's brain tumour started to grow and he became very ill. Alf and Elsie cared for him as long as they could but he was admitted to St Helens Hospital in January 1980 and died about three weeks later on the 17th February 1980. He was only 35 years old and Alf was with him when he died.

Alf and Elsie's last move was to Marine Court in St Leonards, an art-deco apartment block that was built on the seafront and looks like a ship. This is only a short distance from where Alf was born, and here they lived happily until Elsie died suddenly in 1996.

Alf who is very lonely without her still lives there and it was here in August 2001 that he met you, his great granddaughter Selina, when you visited him with your parents.

# 30

## *The Flynns*

### ROBERT JAMES FLYNN—YOUR GRANDFATHER

Robert James Flynn was born in his grandmother's house at 38 Riverdene Edgware on 5th November 1944, he was always known as Bob.

His parents soon moved to a house in Cricklewood very near to the Brent Cross Shopping Centre, but they were an ambitious pair and worked and saved hard to move back to their own home at 91 Riverdene, Edgware.

Bob went to school in Cricklewood and then to Edgware Secondary School, where he was a good pupil and got a quite a few General Certificate of Education O Levels.

He started work as a youth in training for the Post Office Telecommunications and on his first day met Martin Rawlings, who was to become our very close friend and Godfather to both your Uncle Andrew and your father.

Bob was a very gregarious character, having the same sense of humour he had inherited from his grandfather, and he was a very kind man. He had deep blue eyes and could certainly charm the ladies. He was a talented football referee and by 1968 had got as far as refereeing minor league matches all over the south of England, he was ambitious enough to dream of refereeing premier division games and young enough to be able to get that far, but fate had other plans for him.

We were married in April 1966 and our first son Andrew was born in January 1968, We had a few happy years together, but we were never very well suited and the marriage fell apart not long after your father Stuart was born in 1971.

Bob did well working for the post office and eventually became a technical officer, but in 1967 he was diagnosed with a cyst in a cavity of his brain, which gave him seizures and led to mood changes. His illness affected him quite badly and he resigned from the Post Office and worked for private telecommunications companies for several years, keeping his illness a secret from his employers.

He also did some work for a national charity and one day in the summer of 1976 while he was driving he had a seizure and smashed his car into the front of a house. After this he was unable to drive and he lost the will to work so we exchanged roles with me going to work while he stayed at home. We struggled along for a few years although neither of us was very happy, eventually parting in 1978.

Your great-grandparents never forgave me for the divorce and although I do not accept full responsibility for the break-up of the marriage, I can understand their point of view. I made no attempt to see them again after the separation, as I would have been unwelcome.

There was never any bad feeling between your grandfather and me, in fact we were able to get on a lot better once we had parted and we kept in touch until he became too ill. This happened quite suddenly in the autumn of 1979, as up until then everyone had expected him to have an almost normal life expectancy although it did appear that the cyst in his brain was slowly growing and the seizures were happening more often.

He died in February 1980 aged only thirty-five and although I had known for a few weeks that he was dying it was still a dreadful shock to lose someone so young. It was a terrible loss for his two boys when he died, and definitely the waste of a good life.

# Conclusion

✦

## Spring 2003

We come to the end of this family story and unfortunately the Wynn name has not been passed on to the next generation, so our branch will disappear, as have both the Raven and Stack names. There are still direct male descendants of John Grosch, but although they are not from our family, at least his name and bloodline will still continue for another generation.

Writing this history has given me some poignant moments. I now realise how unlucky I am to have missed meeting my grandfather Charles George Wynn by just three years, as his wife and sons spoke of him with such great affection that I am sure I would have loved him. My father often spoke of him and told me how much he would have loved his two granddaughters. I have also become much more conscious of what his generation suffered in the Great War.

The extended family I grew up with were decent hard working people who enjoyed life and, with only one exception, kept to the rules.

Our family did not produce any great minds and no one was famous. Most of your ancestors, including the Flynn family, lived their lives with very few expectations of anything except to work hard to earn enough to eat. In fact this way of life did not alter very much until the end of the Second World War, when my generation was born.

I was fortunate to grow up in a time of real prosperity for all classes if you were prepared to work hard. I do not think the next generations will have as many opportunities for improvement as did mine—how things have changed yet again.

The rest of our recent family history is for your father and uncle to tell you, but as you can see from this history, you have an English lineage, which together with your Spanish blood, you can be as proud of as I am.

Eastbourne—April 2003

William Leslie Wynn
The last male of the Wynn family
in February 2003

# Genealogy Tables

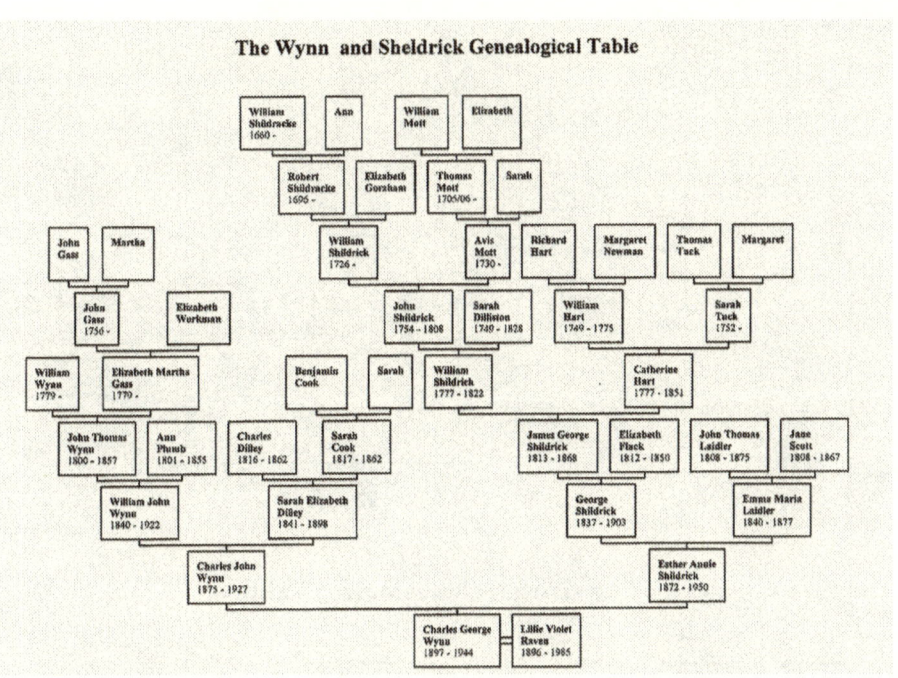

The Wynn and Sheldrick Genealogical Table

## The Raven Genealogical Table

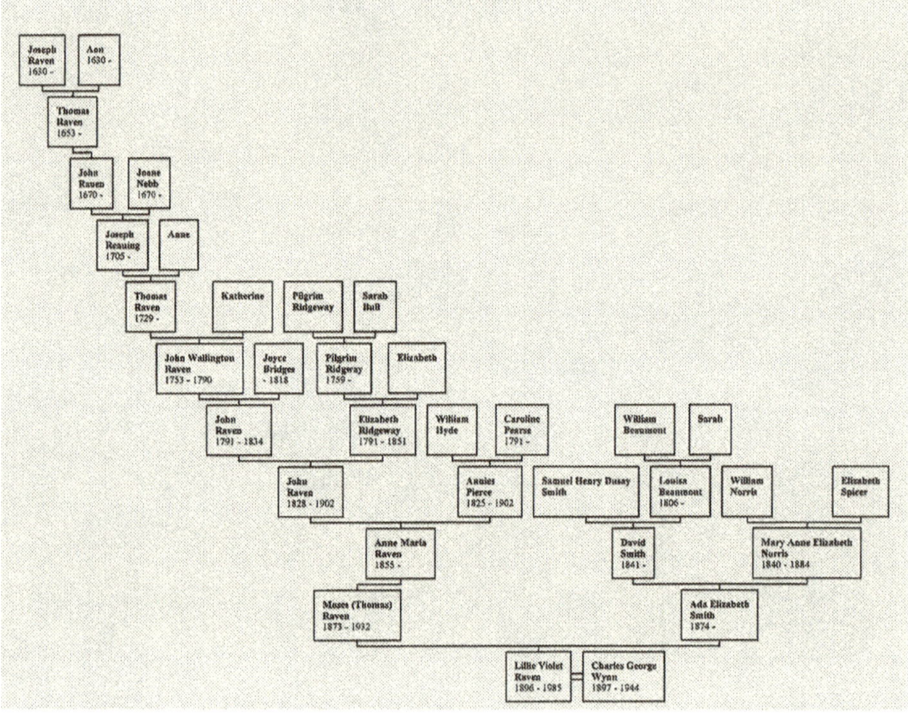

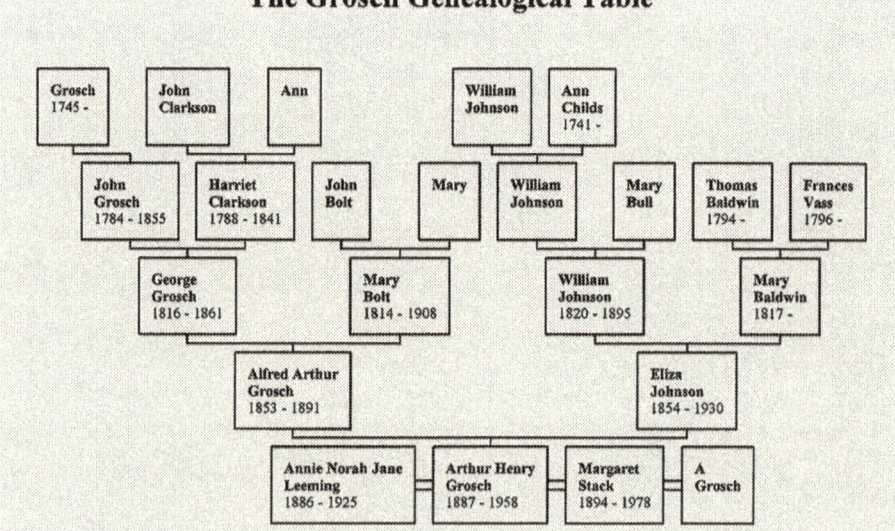

## The Grosch Genealogical Table

# The Stack Genealogical Table

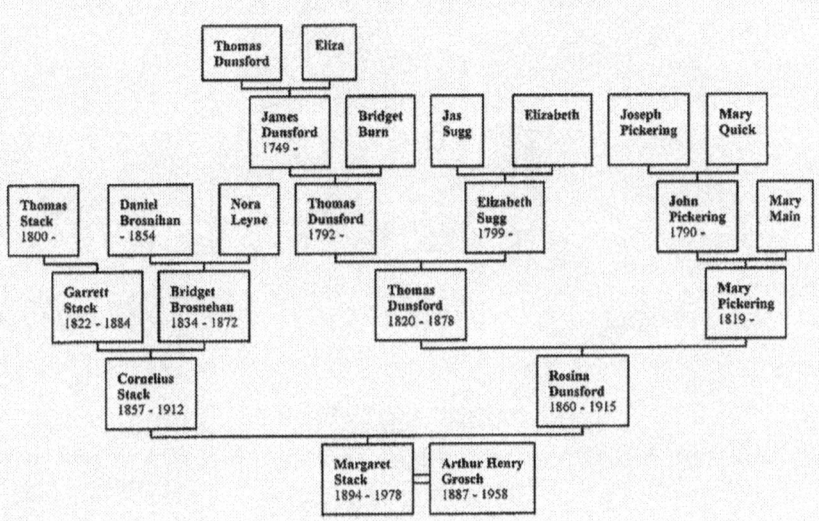

## The Flynn Genealogical Table

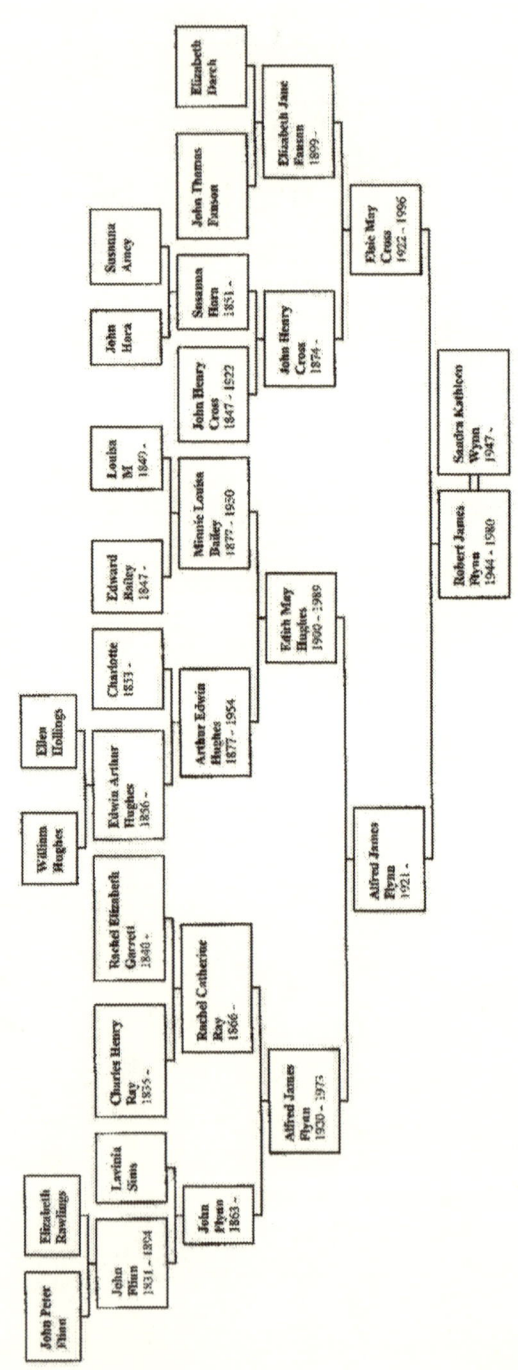

# The English Ancestors of Selina

## GENERATION NO. 1

**Selina Flynn-Elias,** born 25 July 2001 in Hospital de la Plana, Vila-Real, Spain Baptised Christ the King Catholic Church Eastbourne 4th August 2002 The daughter of **Stuart Charles Flynn** and **Maria del Pilar Elias Torregrosa**.

## GENERATION NO. 2

**Stuart Charles Flynn,** born 6 January 1971 in 42 Birch Way Hastings East Sussex. Baptised at Blacklands Church Hastings July 1971. The son of **Robert James Flynn** and **Sandra Kathleen Wynn**. He married **Maria del Pilar Elias Torregrosa** 23 September 2000 in Capella Ermita, Vila-real Spain.
**Maria del Pilar Elias Torregrosa,** born 23 March 1974 in Castellon Spain. The daughter of **Juan Elias Gil** and **Maria Pilar Torregrosa Zapata**.

Child of Stuart Flynn and Maria Torregrosa is:

1. Selina Flynn-Elias, born 25 July 2001 in Hospital de la Plana, Vila-Real, Spain Baptised Christ the King Catholic Church Eastbourne 4th August 2002.

## GENERATION NO. 3

**Robert James Flynn,** born 5 November 1944 in 38 Riverdene, Edgware; died 17 February 1980 in St Helens Hospital, Hastings. The son of **Alfred James Flynn** and **Elsie May Cross**. He married **Sandra Kathleen Wynn** 2 April 1966 in John Keble Church Mill Hill London.
**Sandra Kathleen Wynn,** born 5 April 1947 in Redhill Hospital, Now Edgware General Hospital. The daughter of **Charles Arthur Wynn** and **Kathleen Offord Stack**.

Children of Robert Flynn and Sandra Wynn are:

1.  Andrew James Flynn, born 10 January 1968 in Kingsbury Maternity Hospital Kingsbury London. Baptised at John Keble Church Mill Hill April 21st 1968; met (1) Annie Wickens 1984; met (2) Julie Cornwall 1988 in Brighton; met (3) Wendy Bennett 1999 in Eastbourne.

2.  Stuart Charles Flynn, born 6 January 1971 in 42 Birch Way Hastings East Sussex Baptised at Blacklands Church Hastings July 1971; married Maria del Pilar Elias Torregrosa 23 September 2000 in Capella Ermita, Vila-real Spain.

**Juan Elias Gil** He married **Maria Pilar Torregrosa Zapata.**

Children of Juan Gil and Maria Zapata are:

1.  Yolanda Elias Torregrosa

2.  Maria del Pilar Elias Torregrosa, born 23 March 1974 in Castellon Spain; married Stuart Charles Flynn 23 September 2000 in Capella Ermita, Vila-real Spain.

# GENERATION No. 4

**Alfred James Flynn,** born 29 September 1921 in 13 Alfred St, St Leonards on Sea. The son of **Alfred James Flynn** and **Edith May Hughes**. He married **Elsie May Cross** 24 December 1942 in Hendon.
**Elsie May Cross,** born 25 September 1922 in Medrose St Teath Camelford Cornwall; died 1996 in Hastings. The daughter of **John Henry Cross** and **Elizabeth Jane Fanson**.

Child of Alfred Flynn and Elsie Cross is:

1.  Robert James Flynn, born 5 November 1944 in 38 Riverdene, Edgware; died 17 February 1980 in St Helens Hospital, Hastings; married Sandra Kathleen Wynn 2 April 1966 in John Keble Church Mill Hill London.

**Charles Arthur Wynn,** born 28 May 1924 in 73 Victoria Road, St Pancras; died 5 February 2000 in 31 Langney Green, Eastbourne. The son of **Charles George Wynn** and **Lillie Violet Raven**. He married **Kathleen Offord Stack** 7 September 1946 in John Keble Church Mill Hill London.

**Kathleen Offord Stack,** born 30 May 1925 in 4 Kings Road St Pancras; died 28 February 1998 in 31 Langney Green, Eastbourne. The daughter of **Arthur Henry Grosch** and **Margaret Stack**.

Children of Charles Wynn and Kathleen Stack are:

1. Sandra Kathleen Wynn, born 5 April 1947 in Redhill Hospital, Now Edgware General Hospital; married (1) Robert James Flynn 2 April 1966 in John Keble Church Mill Hill London; married (2) Robert Lewis 28 March 1979 in Eastbourne Register Office.

2. Janice Patricia Wynn, born 21 June 1951 in 54 Fryent Crescent Hendon London; married (1) Nigel Hunt 13 June 1970 in John Keble Church, Mill Hill London; born 17 January 1946 in Crosby Lancashire; married (2) Christopher John Stuart Everett 1 April 2000 in Crawley; born 13 January 1949 in Bexley.

## GENERATION NO. 5

**Alfred James Flynn,** born 1 January 1900 in 2 Hopkins Street, Westminster; died 1973 in Edgware General Hospital. The son of **John Flynn** and **Rachel Catherine Ray**. He married **Edith May Hughes** 4 September 1920 in Cathedral of St John the Evangelist Portsmouth.
**Edith May Hughes,** born 28 November 1900 in 20 Prince of Wales Crescent, St Pancras; died 2 March 1989 in Hastings. The daughter of **Arthur Edwin Hughes** and **Minnie Louisa Bailey**.

Children of Alfred Flynn and Edith Hughes are:

1. Alfred James Flynn, born 29 September 1921 in 13 Alfred St, St Leonards on Sea; married Elsie May Cross 24 December 1942 in Hendon.

2. Patrick Flynn, born 1930; married Maureen.

**John Henry Cross,** born 25 June 1874 in Higher Pengelly, St Teath, Camelford Cornwall. The son of **John Henry Cross** and **Susanna Hora**. He married **Elizabeth Jane Fanson** 29 July 1922 in The Register Office, Camelford.
**Elizabeth Jane Fanson,** born 6 April 1899 in Gooseham Morwinstow Cornwall. The daughter of **John Thomas Fanson** and **Elizabeth Darch**.

Child of John Cross and Elizabeth Fanson is:

1.  Elsie May Cross, born 25 September 1922 in Medrose St Teath Camelford Cornwall; died 1996 in Hastings; married Alfred James Flynn 24 December 1942 in Hendon.

**Charles George Wynn,** born 13 September 1897 in 4 Crescent Place, Tottenham Court St Pancras; died 3 March 1944 in Edgware General Hospital. The son of **Charles John Wynn** and **Esther Annie Shildrick.** He married **Lillie Violet Raven** 4 August 1923 in St Marys Somers Town London.
**Lillie Violet Raven,** born 14 November 1896 in Ballards Buildings Watford; died 17 January 1985 in 63 Deansbrook Road Edgware. The daughter of **Moses (Thomas) Raven** and **Ada Elizabeth Smith.**

Children of Charles Wynn and Lillie Raven are:

1.  Charles Arthur Wynn, born 28 May 1924 in 73 Victoria Road, St Pancras; died 5 February 2000 in 31 Langney Green, Eastbourne; married Kathleen Offord Stack 7 September 1946 in John Keble Church Mill Hill London.

2.  William Leslie Wynn, born 3 May 1928 in 73 Victoria Road, St Pancras.

**Arthur Henry Grosch,** born 13 January 1887 in 88 Gloucester Road St Pancras; died 7 April 1958 in Edgware General Hospital. The son of **Alfred Arthur Grosch** and **Eliza Johnson.** He married **Margaret Stack** 21 April 1926 in St Pancras Register Office.
**Margaret Stack,** born 1 December 1894 in 115 Quinn Buildings, Islington; died 13 January 1978 in St James Hospital Kings Lynn. The daughter of **Cornelius Stack** and **Rosina Dunsford.**

Child of Arthur Grosch and Margaret Stack is:

1.  Kathleen Offord Stack, born 30 May 1925 in 4 Kings Road St Pancras; died 28 February 1998 in 31 Langney Green, Eastbourne; married Charles Arthur Wynn 7 September 1946 in John Keble Church Mill Hill London.

# GENERATION NO. 6

**John Flynn,** born 7 September 1863 in 8 Cross Street Westminster. The son of **John Flinn** and **Lavinia Sims**. He married **Rachel Catherine Ray** 2 September 1888 in St Andrews Church Enfield.

**Rachel Catherine Ray,** born 26 November 1866 in 6 Hasland Street Westminster. The daughter of **Charles Henry Ray** and **Rachel Elizabeth Garrett**.

Children of John Flynn and Rachel Ray are:

1.  Lillie Flynn, born 1890 in Marylebone.

2.  Daisy Flynn, born 1892 in Marylebone.

3.  John Flynn, born 1894 in Marylebone.

4.  Alfred James Flynn, born 1 January 1900 in 2 Hopkins Street, Westminster; died 1973 in Edgware General Hospital; married Edith May Hughes 4 September 1920 in Cathedral of St John the Evangelist Portsmouth.

**Arthur Edwin Hughes,** born 1877 in St Pancras; died 1954 in Hastings. The son of **Edwin Arthur Hughes** and **Charlotte**. He married **Minnie Louisa Bailey**.

**Minnie Louisa Bailey,** born 1877 in Islington Middlesex; died 1950 in Hastings. The daughter of **Edward Bailey** and **Louisa M**.

Children of Arthur Hughes and Minnie Bailey are:

1.  Minnie Rose Hughes, born 1896 in Hastings; married Harry Hughes.

2.  Edith May Hughes, born 28 November 1900 in 20 Prince of Wales Crescent, St Pancras; died 2 March 1989 in Hastings; married Alfred James Flynn 4 September 1920 in Cathedral of St John the Evangelist Portsmouth.

3.  Alfred Sidney Hughes, born 1903.

4.  Ivy Lillian Hughes, born 1905; died 1997; married Jack Jenner.

5.  Edward Alfred Hughes, born 1908 in Hastings; died 2000 in Hastings; married Sylvia.

6.  Horace Percy Hughes, born 1913 in 1999; married (1) Dot; married (2) Elsie.

7.  Joseph William Hughes, born 1917; married (1) Eileen Mungeam; born about. 1935; married (2) Margaret Howe; born 4 February 1934.

8.  Rose Hughes, born 1918 in Hastings; married Alfred Prior; died about. 1995 in Hastings.

**John Henry Cross,** born 1847 in Okehampton Devon; died before 1922. He married **Susanna Hora.**
**Susanna Hora,** born 18 November 1851 in Trelights St Endellion Cornwall. The daughter of **John Hora** and **Susanna Amey.**

Children of John Cross and Susanna Hora are:

1.  Samuel J Cross, born 1872 in Endellion Cornwall.

2.  John Henry Cross, born 25 June 1874 in Higher Pengelly, St Teath, Camelford Cornwall; married Elizabeth Jane Fanson 29 July 1922 in The Register Office, Camelford.

3.  Mary E Cross, born 1875 in St Teath Cornwall.

4.  Alfred Cross, born 1877 in St Teath Cornwall.

5.  Susannah Cross, born 1881 in St Teath Cornwall.

**John Thomas Fanson** He married **Elizabeth Darch.**

Child of John Fanson and Elizabeth Darch is:

1.  Elizabeth Jane Fanson, born 6 April 1899 in Gooseham Morwinstow Cornwall; married (1) Mr Jewell about.1920; married (2) John Henry Cross 29 July 1922 in The Register Office, Camelford.

**Charles John Wynn,** born 12 February 1875 in 5 Torrington Mews St Giles in the Fields; died 21 December 1927 in 199 Dartmouth Park Hill (Whittington Hospital). The son of **William John Wynn** and **Sarah Elizabeth Dilley.** He married **Esther Annie Shildrick** 25 December 1896 in St Giles in the Fields, Middlesex.
**Esther Annie Shildrick,** born 30 April 1872 in 2 Brunswick Buildings, Grays Inn; died 25 July 1950 in St Pancras Hospital. The daughter of **George Shildrick** and **Emma Maria Laidler.**

Children of Charles Wynn and Esther Shildrick are:

1. Charles George Wynn, born 13 September 1897 in 4 Crescent Place, Tottenham Court St Pancras; died 3 March 1944 in Edgware General Hospital; married Lillie Violet Raven 4 August 1923 in St Marys Somers Town London.

2. William Alfred Wynn, born 23 April 1899 in St Pancras; died 20 April 1976 in St Pancras; married Florence May Furnish 4 November 1950 in St Pancras Register Office; born 1897 in Yorkshire; died after 1976.

**Moses (Thomas) Raven,** born 28 January 1873 in Farthing Lane Watford; died 14 January 1932 in 4 Kings Road, St Pancras. Buried in St Pancras Cemetery Finchley. Chapel Ground Grave NO. 470 Section FF. The son of **Anne Maria Raven**. He married **Ada Elizabeth Smith** 19 August 1894 in Oxhey Parish Church. Hertfordshire.
**Ada Elizabeth Smith,** born 14 June 1874 in 18 Eastcourt Road Watford. The daughter of **David Smith** and **Mary Anne Elizabeth Norris**.

Children of Moses Raven and Ada Smith are:

1. Ada Hamerdine Raven, born 4 July 1895 in Clarks Buildings, Watford; died 9 September 1991 in Watford; married George Harding; born 1894 in Watford; died 1949 in Watford.

2. Lillie Violet Raven, born 14 November 1896 in Ballards Buildings Watford; died 17 January 1985 in 63 Deansbrook Road Edgware; married Charles George Wynn 4 August 1923 in St Marys Somers Town London.

3. Edith Dorothy Raven, born 1899 in Watford; died 23 July 1991 in Edgware; married Henry Mark Walker 10 September 1927 in St Pancras Register Office; born 1894; died 31 January 1942 in Edgware. Buried in Hendon park Cemetery Grave No.52638.

4. Beatrice Victoria May Raven, born 9 February 1904 in 63 Cardiff Road, Watford Hertfordshire; died 28 April 1920 in 199 Dartmouth Park Hill. Buried in St Pancras Cemetery Finchley.

5. Arthur Harry Thomas Raven, born 1905 in Watford; died 23 July 1964 in Sutton; married Ivy Doris Stevens; born 1903; died 1971 in Sutton.

6.  Doris Maud Daisy Raven, born 17 June 1907 in 63 Cardiff Road Watford; died 13 January 2002 in Clacton; married Charles James Cullum 25 December 1930 in St Pancras Church; born 1905 in Camden; died 1973 in Enfield.

**Alfred Arthur Grosch,** born 5 June 1853 in 2 Mortimer Market, Saint Pancras; died 18 November 1891 in Gloucester Road St Pancras. The son of **George Grosch** and **Mary Bolt**. He married **Eliza Johnson** 1 April 1877 in St Thomas Portman Square.

**Eliza Johnson,** born 21 January 1854 in Harpenden Lane, Redbourn Herts. died 11 February 1930 in 150 Bathurst Gardens Harlesden. The daughter of **William Johnson** and **Mary Baldwin**.

Children of Alfred Grosch and Eliza Johnson are:

1.  Alfred Lewin Grosch, born 1878; died 1950; married Margaret Ann; born 1880; died 1924.

2.  Ethel L. Grosch, born 31 January 1879; married Mr Gibbons 1904.

3.  William George Grosch, born 1880; died 1947; married Jane Lavender; born 1880; died 1964.

4.  Nellie Grosch, born 1883 in St Pancras; died 1965.

5.  Arthur Henry Grosch, born 13 January 1887 in 88 Gloucester Road St Pancras; died 7 April 1958 in Edgware General Hospital; married (1) Annie Norah Jane Leeming 4 July 1912 in St Pancras Register Office; married (2) Margaret Stack 21 April 1926 in St Pancras Register Office; met (3) A Grosch Aft. 1927.

6.  Frederick Edward Grosch, born 1888; died 1943; married Rosetta Wingrove 1912; born 1888; died 1983.

**Cornelius Stack,** born 1857 in Islington; died 21 October 1912 in St Pancras Infirmary Highgate. The son of **Garrett Stack** and **Bridget Brosnehan**. He married **Rosina Dunsford** 24 July 1883 in Islington Register Office.

**Rosina Dunsford,** born 4 October 1860 in 1 Malt House Mews Marylebone, Middlesex; died 20 February 1915 in Islington Infirmary. The daughter of **Thomas Dunsford** and **Mary Pickering**.

Children of Cornelius Stack and Rosina Dunsford are:

1.  Rosina Stack, born 9 May 1884 in 24 Enkel Street Islington; died September 1896 in Islington.

2.  Florence Stack, born 1886 in Highbury; died Aft. 1891.

3.  Walter Cornelius Stack, born 18 October 1887 in 13 Alma Terrace Islington; died 1 August 1954 in Edgware General Hospital.

4.  Charles Stack, born 1890 in Clerkenwell; died about 1958.

5.  Margaret Stack, born 1 December 1894 in 115 Quinn Buildings, Islington; died 13 January 1978 in St James Hospital Kings Lynn; married Arthur Henry Grosch 21 April 1926 in St Pancras Register Office.

6.  Mary Stack, born 1898 in St Pancras; married Charles William Offord 21 April 1923 in St Pancras Register Office; born 1897.

7.  Samuel Stack, born 1901; died 14 February 1925 in 4 Kings Road, St Pancras.

# GENERATION NO. 7

**John Flinn,** born 1831 in Westminster Baptised St Luke Chelsea 19 September 1832; died June 1894 in Westminster. The son of **John Peter Flinn** and **Elizabeth Rawlings**. He married **Lavinia Sims** 6 February 1859 in St James Westminster. **Lavinia Sims,** born in Westminster.

Children of John Flinn and Lavinia Sims are:

1.  James Flynn, born 1860 in Westminster.

2.  Mary Flynn, born 1862 in Westminster.

3.  John Flynn, born 7 September 1863 in 8 Cross Street Westminster; married Rachel Catherine Ray 2 September 1888 in St Andrews Church Enfield.

4.  Charles Flynn, born 1866 in Westminster.

5.  Annie Flynn, born 1868 Baptised 7 Feb 1869 in St James Westminster.

**Charles Henry Ray,** born 1835 in America. He married **Rachel Elizabeth Garrett,** born 1840 in Westminster.

Children of Charles Ray and Rachel Garrett are:

1.  Emily Ray, born 1863 in Westminster.

2.  Rachel Catherine Ray, born 26 November 1866 in 6 Hasland Street Westminster; married John Flynn 2 September 1888 in St Andrews Church Enfield.

3.  Charles Ray, born 1869 in Westminster.

**Edwin Arthur Hughes,** born 1856 in Baptised 21 Sep 1863 St Pancras. The son of **William Hughes** and **Ellen Hollings**. He married **Charlotte**, born 1853 in Paddington.Children of Edwin Hughes and Charlotte are:

1.  Arthur Edwin Hughes, born 1877 in St Pancras; died 1954 in Hastings; married Minnie Louisa Bailey.

2.  Joseph William Hughes, born 1880 in Smithfield.

3.  Charlotte Hughes, born 1882 in Holloway.

4.  George Hughes, born 1885 in St Pancras.

5.  Florence Hughes, born 1890 in St Pancras.

**Edward Bailey,** born 1847 in Islington Middlesex. He married **Louisa M,** born 1849 in Islington Middlesex.

Children of Edward Bailey and Louisa M are:

1.  Amy E Bailey, born 1868.

2.  Edward A Bailey, born 1871.

3.  Frank Bailey, born 1874.

4.  Arthur Bailey, born 1875.

5.  Minnie Louisa Bailey, born 1877 in Islington Middlesex; died 1950 in Hastings; married Arthur Edwin Hughes.

6.  Louise H Bailey, born 1879.

7.  Rose E Bailey, born 1881.

**John Hora** He married **Susanna Amey.**

Child of John Hora and Susanna Amey is:

1.  Susanna Hora, born 18 November 1851 in Trelights St Endellion Cornwall; married John Henry Cross.

**William John Wynn,** born 10 April 1840 in 25 Berners Mews Marylebone; died 11 December 1922 in 4 Kings Road St Pancras. The son of **John Thomas Wynn** and **Ann Plumb**. He married **Sarah Elizabeth Dilley** 21 April 1862 in St Mary Magdalene St Pancras.
**Sarah Elizabeth Dilley,** born 3 April 1841 in Pleasant Garden Islington London. Baptised St Pancras Old Church 24 April 1841; died 3 November 1898 in 30 Keppel Mews North. The daughter of **Charles Dilley** and **Sarah Cook**.

Children of William Wynn and Sarah Dilley are:

1.  William Charles Wynn, born 3 January 1863 Baptised St Pancras Old Church 16 February 1863; died 10 February 1867 in 8 York Buildings Chalton St, Somers Town.

2.  Sarah Ann Wynn, born 11 March 1865 in 7 Churchway St Pancras Baptised at St Pancras Old Church 3rd April 1865; died 16 February 1930 in St Pancras; married James Richard Embleton 4 August 1884 in St Giles in the Fields, Middlesex; born 12 January 1860 in 28 Church Way Somers town. Baptised 16 Jan 1865 St Pancras Old church; died 22 May 1934 in St Pancras.

3.  Thomas John Wynn, born 10 February 1868 Baptised St Pancras Old Church.

4.  Phoebe Wynn, born 29 April 1870 in 1 Christopher Place Somers Town. Baptised 16th May 1870 at St Pancras Old Church; died 21 May 1937 in St Pancras; married (1) James Henry Collins 6 August 1888 in St Giles in the Fields, Middlesex; born 1863 in Islington; died 27 November 1907 in St Pancras; married (2) Oliver Samuel Luke Evans 3 October 1911 in Holborn Register Office; born 1877 in Islington Infirmary; died 30 March 1935 in Manor Park. Grave No 381 Manor Park Cemetery.

5.  Watkin Alfred Wynn, born 3 February 1873 in St Giles in the Fields; died 20 March 1875 in 5 Torrington Mews, St Giles in the Fields.

6.  Charles John Wynn, born 12 February 1875 in 5 Torrington Mews St Giles in the Fields; died 21 December 1927 in 199 Dartmouth Park Hill (Whittington Hospital); married Esther Annie Shildrick 25 December 1896 in St Giles in the Fields, Middlesex.

7.  Alfred Wynn, born 1879 in St Giles in the Fields.

**George Shildrick,** born 1837 in Bottisham Cambridge. Christened 21 May 1837; died 30 November 1903 in 7 Penton Place, Clerkenwell. The son of **James George Shildrick** and **Elizabeth Flack**. He married **Emma Maria Laidler** 13 July 1868 in St Pancras Church.
**Emma Maria Laidler,** born 12 May 1840 in 1 Rawston Place Clerkenwell; died 6 March 1877 in Lambeth Workhouse Infirmary. The daughter of **John Thomas Laidler** and **Jane Scott**.

Children of George Shildrick and Emma Laidler are:

1.  Emily Sheldrick, born 1870 in St Pancras; died in Paddington. Buried in Mill Hill Cemetery Milespit Hill.

2.  William Sheldrick, born March 1871; died 1872.

3.  Esther Annie Shildrick, born 30 April 1872 in 2 Brunswick Buildings, Grays Inn; died 25 July 1950 in St Pancras Hospital; married Charles John Wynn 25 December 1896 in St Giles in the Fields, Middlesex.

4.  Harriet Shildrick, born August 1873; died 20 October 1873 in 2 Brunswick Buildings, St Pancras.

5.  George Sheldrick, born January 1875; died 20 March 1875 in 27 Argyle Street, St Pancras.

**Anne Maria Raven,** born 7 April 1855 in Flint Hall Bushey. Baptised 18 Jan 1856. The daughter of **John Raven** and **Annies Pierce**.

Child of Anne Maria Raven is:

1.  Moses (Thomas) Raven, born 28 January 1873 in Farthing Lane Watford; died 14 January 1932 in 4 Kings Road, St Pancras. Buried in St Pancras Cemetery Finchley. chapel Ground Grave NO. 470 Section FF; married (1) Ada Elizabeth Smith 19 August 1894 in Oxhey Parish Church. Hertfordshire; met (2) Beatrice about. 1910.

**David Smith,** born 27 January 1841 in Aldenham Wood Aldenham Bushey. The son of **Samuel Henry Dusay Smith** and **Louisa Beaumont**. He married **Mary Anne Elizabeth Norris** 12 April 1869 in Aldenham Church.
**Mary Anne Elizabeth Norris,** born 5 July 1840 in High Street, Watford; died before. 1884. The daughter of **William Norris** and **Elizabeth Spicer**.

Children of David Smith and Mary Norris are:

1. David G Smith, born 1872.

2. Ada Elizabeth Smith, born 14 June 1874 in 18 Eastcourt Road Watford; married Moses (Thomas) Raven 19 August 1894 in Oxhey Parish Church. Hertfordshire.

3. Arthur S Smith, born 1877.

4. Harry J Smith, born 1879.

**George Grosch,** born 1816 in London; died 25 September 1861 in 6 Warren St, St Pancras. The son of **John Grosch** and **Harriet Clarkson**. He married **Mary Bolt** 25 May 1841 in St George, Hanover Square.
**Mary Bolt,** born 13 February 1814 in Cheriton Bishop, Devon; died 10 February 1908 in St Pancras Infirmary. The daughter of **John Bolt** and **Mary**.

Children of George Grosch and Mary Bolt are:

1. George Lewin Grosch, born 14 September 1842 in 1 Mansfield Place, Baptised 23 October 1842 St Pancras Old Church; died 1889; married Martha Sarah Burgan 1865; born 1847.

2. Reuben John Grosch, born 1844 Baptised 3 November 1844 St Pancras Old Church; died 1890; married Sarah Ann Jones 15 October 1866 in St Pancras Old Church; born 1850 in Marylebone.

3. Selina Mary Grosch, born 1848 Baptised 11 June 1848 St Pancras Old Church; married Robert Grant 15 June 1873 in St Pancras Old Church; born 1838 in Marylebone.

4. Frederick Allen Grosch, born 1850 Baptised 15 December 1850 St Pancras Old Church; died 1933; married Eileen Maria Higginson 1877; born 1857; died 1942.

5.   Alfred Arthur Grosch, born 5 June 1853 in 2 Mortimer Market, Saint Pancras; died 18 November 1891 in Gloucester Road St Pancras; married Eliza Johnson 1 April 1877 in St Thomas Portman Square.

6.   Teresa Malvina Grosch, born 1856 in St Pancras; married William Hall 1878 in St Pancras; born 1854 in Holloway.

7.   Herbert Henry Grosch, born 5 August 1858 in 2 Mortimer Market. St Pancras; died 1929; married (1) Mary Jane Hayes 1888 in St Pancras; born 1864; died 1893; married (2) Elisabeth Hayes 1895 in St Pancras; born 1867; died 1944.

**William Johnson,** born 1820 Baptised 18 November 1821, Redbourn Herts. died 8 March 1895 in St Albans Workhouse. The son of **William Johnson** and **Mary Bull**. He married **Mary Baldwin** 18 October 1843 in St Albans.
**Mary Baldwin,** born 22 June 1817 Baptised 22 June 1817 in Redbourn Herts. The daughter of **Thomas Baldwin** and **Frances Vass**.

Children of William Johnson and Mary Baldwin are:

1.   Elizabeth Johnson, born 1844 in Redbourn Herts.

2.   John Johnson, born 1850 in Redbourn Herts.

3.   Fanny Johnson, born 1852 in Redbourn Herts.

4.   Eliza Johnson, born 21 January 1854 in Harpenden Lane, Redbourn Herts. died 11 February 1930 in 150 Bathurst Gardens Harlesden; married Alfred Arthur Grosch 1 April 1877 in St Thomas Portman Square.

5.   Ann Johnson, born 1856 in Redbourn Herts.

6.   Rose Johnson, born 1858 in Redbourn Herts.

**Garrett Stack,** born 1822 in Ireland; died 12 February 1884 in Islington Infirmary. The son of **Thomas Stack**. He married **Bridget Brosnehan** 10 December 1854 in Catholic Church of St John the Evangelist, Islington.
**Bridget Brosnehan,** born 1834 in Kerry, Ireland; died 9 March 1872 in 5 Lees Court Islington. The daughter of **Daniel Brosnehan** and **Nora Leyne**.

Child of Garrett Stack and Bridget Brosnehan is:

    a.    Cornelius Stack, born 1857 in Islington; died 21 October 1912 in St Pancras Infirmary Highgate; married Rosina Dunsford 24 July 1883 in Islington Register Office.

**Thomas Dunsford,** born 1820 Baptised 19 September 1820. St Mary Major Exeter; died 9 March 1878 in 119 Carlisle St Marylebone. The son of **Thomas Dunsford** and **Elizabeth Sugg**. He married **Mary Pickering** 22 September 1839 in St Marys Portsea Hampshire.
**Mary Pickering,** born 1819 Baptised 11 July 1819 St Marys Portsea Hampshire. The daughter of **John Pickering** and **Mary Main**.

Child of Thomas Dunsford and Mary Pickering is:

    1.    Rosina Dunsford, born 4 October 1860 in 1 Malt House Mews Marylebone, Middlesex; died 20 February 1915 in Islington Infirmary; married Cornelius Stack 24 July 1883 in Islington Register Office.

# GENERATION NO. 8

**John Peter Flinn** He married **Elizabeth Rawlings** 4 May 1823 in St James Westminster.

Children of John Flinn and Elizabeth Rawlings are:

    1.    John Flinn, born 1831 in Westminster Baptised St Luke Chelsea 19 September 1832; died June 1894 in Westminster; married Lavinia Sims 6 February 1859 in St James Westminster.

    2.    Lucy Flinn, born 1834 Baptised 21 February 1834 St James Westminster.

**William Hughes** He married **Ellen Hollings** 25 June 1854 in St Martin in the Fields Westminster.

Child of William Hughes and Ellen Hollings is:

    1.    Edwin Arthur Hughes, born 1856 Baptised 21 Sep 1863 St Pancras; married Charlotte.

**John Thomas Wynn,** born 14 October 1800 Baptised 23 November 1800 at St Luke Old Street Finsbury; died 2 November 1857 in 6 Cottage Place Grays Inn. St. Pancras. The son of **William Wynn** and **Elizabeth Martha Gass**. He married **Ann Plumb** 22 September 1823 in St James Paddington.

**Ann Plumb,** born 1801; died 5 November 1855 in 6 Cottage Place Grays Inn. St. Pancras.

Children of John Wynn and Ann Plumb are:

1.  Ann Elizabeth Wynn, born 1825 Baptised 31 July 1825 St Mary St Marylebone Rd.

2.  Watkin William Wynn, born 1827 Baptised 4 October 1827 St Mary St Marylebone Rd.

3.  Eliza Wynn, born 1830.

4.  John Wynn, born 1833.

5.  Thomas Wynn, born 1838.

6.  William John Wynn, born 10 April 1840 in 25 Berners Mews Marylebone; died 11 December 1922 in 4 Kings Road St Pancras; married Sarah Elizabeth Dilley 21 April 1862 in St Mary Magdalene St Pancras.

**Charles Dilley,** born 1816 in Old Church St Pancras; died after 1862. He married **Sarah Cook** 28 February 1836 in St Leonards Shoreditch.

**Sarah Cook,** born 1817 in Oxford; died after 1862. The daughter of **Benjamin Cook** and **Sarah**.

Children of Charles Dilley and Sarah Cook are:

1.  Susannah Dilley, born 1839 Baptised St Pancras Old Church 30 November 1844.

2.  Sarah Elizabeth Dilley, born 3 April 1841 in Pleasant Garden Islington London. Baptised St Pancras Old Church 24 April 1841; died 3 November 1898 in 30 Keppel Mews North; married William John Wynn 21 April 1862 in St Mary Magdalene St Pancras.

3.  John Dilley, born 16 March 1844 Baptised St Pancras Old Church Baptised 25 March 1844; died before 1851.

4.  Emma Dilley, born 10 November 1844 Baptised St Pancras Old Church 30 November 1844.

5.  Charles Samuel Dilley, born 20 February 1847 in 7 Cheney St Kings Cross. Baptised 4 January 1849 St Pancras Old Church; married Mary; born 1853 in Somers Town.

6.  Thomas William Dilley, born 17 December 1848 Baptised St Pancras Old Church 4 January 1849; married Ellen.

7.  Joseph Dilley, born 30 June 1850 Baptised in St Pancras Old Church 5 September 1850; died before 1851.

8.  James Robert Dilley, born 1 November 1851 Baptised St Pancras Old Church 20 November 1851.

9.  Elizabeth Dilley, born 29 December 1852 Baptised St Pancras Old Church 15 January 1853; died 2 February 1853.

10. Caroline Dilley, born 2 November 1853 Baptised St Pancras Old Church 19 November 1853.

11. William Dilley, born 30 December 1855 Baptised St Pancras Old Church 19 January 1856; married Sarah.

12. James Dilley, born 11 April 1858 Baptised St Pancras Old Church 29 April 1858.

13. Alfred Dilley, born 23 February 1860 in 3 Red Lion Passage Camden Town, Baptised St Pancras Old Church 15 March 1860.

**James George Shildrick,** born 1813 in Bottisham Cambridge Baptised 13 June 1813; died before 1868. The son of **William Shildrick** and **Catherine Hart**. He married **Elizabeth Flack** 5 January 1837 in Bottisham, Cambridge.
**Elizabeth Flack,** born 1812; died 26 July 1850 in Bottisham Cambridge.

Children of James Shildrick and Elizabeth Flack are:

1.  George Shildrick, born 1837 in Bottisham Cambridge. Christened 21 May 1837; died 30 November 1903 in 7 Penton Place, Clerkenwell; married (1) Emma Maria Laidler 13 July 1868 in St Pancras Church; married (2) Emily Dean 15 March 1882 in St Pancras Register Office.

2.  Susanna Flack Shildrick, born 1838 in Bottisham Cambridge. Baptised 16 June 1839.

3.  Harriet Elizabeth Shildrick, born 9 March 1843 in Bottisham Cambridge. Baptised 9 April 1843.

4.  William Shildrick, born 1847 in Bottisham Cambridge. Baptised 30 May 1847.

5.  Lucy Ann Shildrick, born 1847 in Bottisham Cambridge. Baptised 30 May 1847.

6.  David Shildrick, born 1849.

**John Thomas Laidler,** born 1808 in Berwick on Tweed Northumberland; died 21 November 1875 in St Pancras Workhouse. He married **Jane Scott.**
**Jane Scott,** born 1808; died 27 March 1867 in 2 Brunswick Buildings Grays Inn.

Children of John Laidler and Jane Scott are:

1.  Emma Maria Laidler, born 12 May 1840 in 1 Rawston Place Clerkenwell; died 6 March 1877 in Lambeth Workhouse Infirmary; married George Shildrick 13 July 1868 in St Pancras Church.

2.  Sarah Laidler, born 1843 in Clerkenwell.

3.  John Laidler, born 1846 in Islington.

4.  Joseph Laidler, born 1850 in St Luke.

**John Raven,** born 1828 in Waddesden Buckinghamshire Baptised 24 Aug 1828; died 17 November 1902 in Watford Union Infirmary. The son of **John Raven** and **Elizabeth Ridgeway**. He married **Annies Pierce** 15 August 1851 in Oxhey Parish Church. Hertfordshire.
**Annies Pierce,** born 1825 in Baptised in St John the Baptist Church Boddington Northampton on 15 May 1825; died 25 February 1902 in 44 Ballards Buildings Watford. The daughter of **William Hyde** and **Caroline Pearse**.

Children of John Raven and Annies Pierce are:

1.  Cornelius Raven, born 1852 in Bushey, Baptised 8 February 1852; married Jane; born 1856 in Moccas, Hereford.

2.  Olive Raven, born 1852 in Watford; died 1854 in Flint Hall Bushey.

3.  David Raven, born 1855.

4. Anne Maria Raven, born 7 April 1855 in Flint Hall Bushey Baptised 18 Jan 1856; met (2) Frederick Atkins; married (3) Henry Aldridge 13 November 1886 in Watford Register Office.

5. Levi Tennant Raven, born 1857 in Watford Baptised at St Marys Watford 11 November 1864; died 12 December 1937 in Radlett Road Watford; married Elizabeth; born 1847 in Northampton.

6. Carolina Raven, born 1860 in Watford Baptised at St Marys Watford 4 August 1860; died before 1881.

7. Cornelia Raven, born 1860 in Watford; died 14 August 1860 in 4 Ballards Buildings, Watford.

8. Selina Raven, born 1861 in Watford Baptised at St Marys Watford 11 November 1864; married Jesse Carpenter 28 August 1887 in St Marys Watford Hertfordshire; born 25 January 1863 in Watford Baptised at St Marys Watford.

9. John Albert Raven, born 1864 in Watford Baptised at St Marys Watford 11 November 1864; married Elizabeth Walker.

10. Moses Raven, born 1865 in Watford; died 9 July 1866 in 4 Ballards Buildings, Watford.

11. Amadine Raven, born 12 May 1867 in 4 Ballards Buildings Watford; died before 1871.

**Samuel Henry Dusay Smith** He married **Louisa Beaumont** 15 February 1828 in Aldenham Church.
**Louisa Beaumont,** born 1806 Baptised 12 October 1806 at Aldenham. The daughter of **William Beaumont** and **Sarah**.

Child of Samuel Smith and Louisa Beaumont is:

1. David Smith, born 27 January 1841 in Aldenham Wood Aldenham Bushey; married (1) Jane George; married (2) Mary Anne Elizabeth Norris 12 April 1869 in Aldenham Church.

**William Norris** He married **175. Elizabeth Spicer**.

Child of William Norris and Elizabeth Spicer is:

1.  Mary Anne Elizabeth Norris, born 5 July 1840 in High Street, Watford; died before 1884; married David Smith 12 April 1869 in Aldenham Church.

**John Grosch,** born circa 1784 in Mainz Germany; died 28 February 1855 in 5 Francis Street St Pancras. The son of **Herr Grosch**. He married **Harriet Clarkson** 1807 in St George, Hanover Square.
**Harriet Clarkson,** born 1788 Baptised 8 May 1788 St Andrew Holborn; died 1 March 1841 in 5 Francis Street St Pancras. The daughter of **John Clarkson** and **Ann**.

Children of John Grosch and Harriet Clarkson are:

1.  William Henry Grosch, born 1809 in St Anne's, Middlesex; died 7 September 1889 in Islington Infirmary; married Ann Hariott Holder; born 1808; died 1852.

2.  John Grosch, born 1813; died 1889; married Mary Ann; born 1814; died 21 September 1871 in 49 Roman Road, Islington.

3.  George Grosch, born 1816 in London; died 25 September 1861 in 6 Warren St, St Pancras; married Mary Bolt 25 May 1841 in St George, Hanover Square.

4.  Mary Grosch, born 1820.

5.  Hariott Grosch, born 1822; died 1842.

6.  Charles Grosch, born 1827; died 23 November 1869 in Marylebone Workhouse; married Sarah Parkes 2 June 1850 in St Pancras Old Church; born 1829; died 1898.

7.  Charlotte Grosch, born 1829; died 1852.

**John Bolt** He married **179. Mary**.

Child of John Bolt and Mary is:

1.  Mary Bolt, born 13 February 1814 in Cheriton Bishop, Devon; died 10 February 1908 in St Pancras Infirmary; married George Grosch 25 May 1841 in St George, Hanover Square.

**William Johnson** The son of **William Johnson** and **Ann Childs**. He married **Mary Bull** 29 November 1813 in Redbourn Hertford.

Child of William Johnson and Mary Bull is:

1.  William Johnson, born 1820 Baptised 18 November 1821, Redbourn Herts. died 8 March 1895 in St Albans Workhouse; married Mary Baldwin 18 October 1843 in St Albans.

**Thomas Baldwin,** born 1794. He married **Frances Vass** 26 August 1816 in Redbourn Hertford.
**Frances Vass,** born 1796 in South Mimms.

Children of Thomas Baldwin and Frances Vass are:

1.  Mary Baldwin, born 22 June 1817 Baptised 22 June 1817 in Redbourn Herts. married William Johnson 18 October 1843 in St Albans.

2.  Elizabeth Baldwin, born 6 February 1820.

3.  John Baldwin, born 24 February 1822.

4.  Fanny Baldwin, born 1 August 1824.

5.  Thomas Baldwin, born 1825 in Redbourn Herts.

6.  Susan Baldwin, born 12 October 1828.

7.  Hannah Baldwin, born 21 August 1831.

8.  William Baldwin, born 2 December 1832.

9.  Eliza Baldwin, born 29 March 1835 in Redbourn Herts.

10. George Baldwin, born 1839 in Redbourn Herts.

**Thomas Stack,** born circa 1800 in Kerry Ireland.

Child of Thomas Stack is:

1.   Garrett Stack, born 1822 in Ireland; died 12 February 1884 in Islington Infirmary; married Bridget Brosnehan 10 December 1854 in Catholic Church of St John the Evangelist, Islington.

**Daniel Brosnehan** died before 1854. He married **Nora Leyne** 26 November 1828 in Kilcummin Parish, Kerry.

Children of Daniel Brosnehan and Nora Leyne are:

1.   Bridget Brosnehan, born 1834 in Kerry, Ireland; died 9 March 1872 in 5 Lees Court Islington; married Garrett Stack 10 December 1854 in Catholic Church of St John the Evangelist, Islington.

2.   Cornelius Brosnehan, born 1828 in Killorglin, Kerry; married Catherine Clifford.

**Thomas Dunsford,** born 1792 Baptised 8 April 1792 St Mary Steps Exeter. He was the son of **James Dunsford** and **Bridget Burn**. He married **Elizabeth Sugg** 18 August 1817 in St Mary Major Exeter.
**Elizabeth Sugg,** born 29 September 1799 Baptised 2 December 1799 Bow Now Mint Meeting or Georges Meeting House Presbyterian Exeter. The daughter of **Jas Sugg** and **Elizabeth**.

Children of Thomas Dunsford and Elizabeth Sugg are:

1.   James Sugg Dunsford, born 1818 Baptised 4 August 1918 St Mary Major Exeter.

2.   Thomas Dunsford, born 1820 Baptised 19 September 1820. St Mary Major Exeter; died 9 March 1878 in 119 Carlisle St Marylebone; married Mary Pickering 22 September 1839 in St Marys Portsea Hampshire.

3.   Elizabeth Dunsford, born 1825 Baptised 11 September 1825 St Mary Major Exeter.

**John Pickering,** born 1790 Baptised 24 October 1790 St Marys Portsea Hampshire. The son of **Joseph Pickering** and **Mary Quick**. He married **Mary Main** 28 April 1811 in St Marys Portsea Hampshire.

Child of John Pickering and Mary Main is:

1.  Mary Pickering, born 1819 Baptised 11 July 1819 St Marys Portsea Hampshire; married Thomas Dunsford 22 September 1839 in St Marys Portsea Hampshire.

# GENERATION NO. 9

**William Wynn,** born circa. 1779. He married **Elizabeth Martha Gass** 31 March 1799 in St Giles Cripplegate.
**Elizabeth Martha Gass,** born 13 September 1779 Baptised 3 October 1779 at St Luke Old Street Finsbury. The daughter of **John Gass** and **Elizabeth Workman**.

Children of William Wynn and Elizabeth Gass are:

1.  John Thomas Wynn, born 14 October 1800 Baptised 23 November 1800 at St Luke Old Street Finsbury; died 2 November 1857 in 6 Cottage Place Grays Inn. St. Pancras; married Ann Plumb 22 September 1823 in St James Paddington.

2.  William George Wynn, born 1803 Baptised 30 January 1803 Saint Giles Cripplegate.

3.  Sophia Wynn, born 1807 Baptised 6 September 1807, St Giles Cripplegate.

4.  Caroline Wynn, born 1808 Baptised 20 December 1808, St Giles Cripplegate.

**Benjamin Cook** He married **Sarah.**

Child of Benjamin Cook and Sarah is:

1.  Sarah Cook, born 1817 in Oxford; died Aft. 1862; married Charles Dilley 28 February 1836 in St Leonards Shoreditch.

**William Shildrick,** born 29 September 1777 in Bottisham Cambridge; died 1822 in Bottisham Cambridge. The son of **John Shildrick** and **Sarah Dilliston**. He married **Catherine Hart** 12 August 1800 in Bottisham, Cambridge.
**Catherine Hart,** born 14 December 1777 in Stow Cum Quy Cambridge; died Aft. 1851. The daughter of **William Hart** and **Sarah Tuck**.

Children of William Shildrick and Catherine Hart are:

1. James George Shildrick, born 1813 in Bottisham Cambridge Baptised 13 June 1813; died before 1868; married Elizabeth Flack 5 January 1837 in Bottisham, Cambridge.

2. Thomas Shildrick, born 1815 in Bottisham Cambridge. Baptised 11 June 1815; died 1815 in Buried in Holy Trinity Bottisham Cambridge.

**John Raven,** born 1791 in Waddesden Buckinghamshire Baptised 22 May 1791; died 13 April 1834 in Waddesden Buckinghamshire. The son of **John Wallington Raven** and **Joyce Bridges**. He married **Elizabeth Ridgeway** 10 April 1814 in Puttenham Hertford.
**Elizabeth Ridgeway,** born 1791 in Buckinghamshire Baptised Waddesden 2 June 1793; died Aft. 1851. The daughter of **Pilgrim Ridgway** and **Elizabeth**.

Children of John Raven and Elizabeth Ridgeway are:

1. Thomas Raven, born 1814 in Waddesden Buckinghamshire Baptised 19 June 1814; died December 1894 in Watford.

2. Mary Raven, born 1817 in Waddesden Buckinghamshire Baptised 20 Jul 1817.

3. Sarah Raven, born 1822 in Waddesden Buckinghamshire Baptised 17 November 1822.

4. Joyce Raven, born 1825 in Waddesden Buckinghamshire Baptised 31 Jul 1825; married Thomas Stratfield 5 September 1847 in Tring, Hertfordshire.

5. John Raven, born 1828 in Waddesden Buckinghamshire Baptised 24 Aug 1828; died 17 November 1902 in Watford Union Infirmary; married Annies Pierce 15 August 1851 in Oxhey Parish Church. Hertfordshire.

6. Herodias Raven, born 1831 in Waddesden Buckinghamshire Baptised 17 July 1831.

**William Hyde** He met **Caroline Pearse** born 1791 in Greatworth Northamptonshire.

Child of William Hyde and Caroline Pearse is:

1.   Annies Pierce, born 1825 Baptised in St John the Baptist Church Boddington Northampton on 15 May 1825; died 25 February 1902 in 44 Ballards Buildings Watford; married John Raven 15 August 1851 in Oxhey Parish Church.

**William Beaumont** He married **Sarah.**

Child of William Beaumont and Sarah is:

1.   Louisa Beaumont, born 1806 Baptised 12 October 1806 at Aldenham; married Samuel Henry Dusay Smith 15 February 1828 in Aldenham Church.

**Herr Grosch,** born circa 1745 in Mainz Germany.

Children of Herr Grosch are:

1.   George Grosch, born circa 1770 in Hannover; died in America.

2.   William Henry Grosch, born circa 1780 in Mainz Germany; married Kate Eliza 1805; born 1788; died 1856.

3.   John Grosch, born circa 1784 in Mainz Germany; died 28 February 1855 in 5 Francis Street St Pancras; married Harriet Clarkson 1807 in St George, Hanover Square.

**John Clarkson** He married **Ann.**

Child of John Clarkson and Ann is:

1.   Harriet Clarkson, born 1788 in Baptised 8 May 1788 St Andrew Holborn; died 1 March 1841 in 5 Francis Street St Pancras; married John Grosch 1807 in St George, Hanover Square.

**William Johnson** He married **Ann Childs** 13 May 1762 in Redbourn Hertford.
**Ann Childs,** born 1741 in Redbourn Herts.

Child of William Johnson and Ann Childs is:

1.   William Johnson married Mary Bull 29 November 1813 in Redbourn Hertford.

**James Dunsford,** born 1749 Baptised 30 January 1749 St Thomas the Apostle Exeter. The son of **Thomas Dunsford** and **Eliza**. He married **Bridget Burn** 27 May 1780 in Okham, Surrey.

Child of James Dunsford and Bridget Burn is:

1.   Thomas Dunsford, born 1792 Baptised 8 April 1792 St Mary Steps Exeter; married Elizabeth Sugg 18 August 1817 in St Mary Major Exeter.

**Jas Sugg** He married **Elizabeth.**

Child of Jas Sugg and Elizabeth is:

1.   Elizabeth Sugg, born 29 September 1799 Baptised 2 December 1799 Bow Now Mint Meeting or Georges Meeting House Presbyterian Exeter; married Thomas Dunsford 18 August 1817 in St Mary Major Exeter.

**Joseph Pickering** He married **Mary Quick** 15 April 1784 in St Marys Portsea Hampshire.

Children of Joseph Pickering and Mary Quick are:

1.   Elizabeth Pickering, born 1786 Baptised 25 September 1786 St Marys Portsea Hampshire.

2.   Benjamin Pickering, born 1788 Baptised 26 October 1788 St Marys Portsea Hampshire.

3.   John Pickering, born 1790 Baptised 24 October 1790 St Marys Portsea Hampshire; married Mary Main 28 April 1811 in St Marys Portsea Hampshire.

# GENERATION NO. 10

**John Gass,** born 1756 Baptised 4 April 1756, St Luke Finsbury. The son of **John Gass** and **Martha**. He married **Elizabeth Workman** 12 September 1781 in St Dunstan, Stepney.

Children of John Gass and Elizabeth Workman are:

1. Elizabeth Martha Gass, born 13 September 1779 Baptised 3 October 1779 at St Luke Old Street Finsbury; married William Wynn 31 March 1799 in St Giles Cripplegate.

2. Sarah Gass, born 1781 Baptised 21 October 1781 St Luke Old St Finsbury.

3. John Gass, born 1783 Baptised 23 March 1783 St Luke Old St Finsbury.

4. William Gass, born 1785 Baptised 1 April 1785 St Luke Old St Finsbury.

5. James Gass, born 1791 Baptised 10 July 1791 St Luke Old St Finsbury.

**John Shildrick,** born 1754 in Bottisham Cambridge. Baptised 2 June 1754; died 1808 in Bottisham Cambridge. The son of **William Shildrick** and **Avis Mott**. He married **Sarah Dilliston** 12 November 1776 in Bottisham, Cambridge. **Sarah Dilliston,** born 1749; died 1828 in Buried in Bottisham.

Children of John Shildrick and Sarah Dilliston are:

1. William Shildrick, born 29 September 1777 in Bottisham Cambridge; died 1822 in Bottisham Cambridge; married Catherine Hart 12 August 1800 in Bottisham, Cambridge.

2. Agnes Shildrick, born 1780 in Bottisham Cambridge. Baptised 23 February 1780.

3. Thomas Reve Shildrick, born 1783 in Bottisham Cambridge. Baptised 6 February 1783.

4. Lucy Reeve Shildrick, born 1789 in Bottisham Cambridge. Baptised 19 April 1789; died 1807 in Bottisham.

5.  Rebecca Shildrick, born 1789 in Bottisham Cambridge. Baptised 11 December 1789; married John Hoy 22 October 1805 in Bottisham, Cambridge.

**William Hart,** born 22 May 1749 in Bottisham Cambridge; died 23 May 1775 in Stow Cum Quy Cambridge. The son of **Richard Hart** and **Margaret Newman**. He married **Sarah Tuck**.
**Sarah Tuck,** born 16 February 1752 in Stow Cum Quy Cambridge. The daughter of **Thomas Tuck** and **Margaret**.

Child of William Hart and Sarah Tuck is:

1.  Catherine Hart, born 14 December 1777 in Stow Cum Quy Cambridge; died after 1851; married William Shildrick 12 August 1800 in Bottisham, Cambridge.

**John Wallington Raven,** born 1753 in Waddesden Buckinghamshire Baptised 15 July 1753; died 1790 in Waddesden Buckinghamshire. The son of **Thomas Raven** and **Katherine**. He married **Joyce Bridges** 28 May 1776 in Waddesden.
**Joyce Bridges** died 29 September 1818 in Buried in Waddesden.

Children of John Raven and Joyce Bridges are:

1.  Joseph Raven, born 1788 in Waddesden Buckinghamshire Baptised 24 Feb 1788.

2.  Mary Raven, born 1788 in Waddesden Buckinghamshire Baptised 24 Feb 1788.

3.  John Raven, born 1791 in Waddesden Buckinghamshire Baptised 22 May 1791; died 13 April 1834 in Waddesden Buckinghamshire; married Elizabeth Ridgeway 10 April 1814 in Puttenham Hertford.

**Pilgrim Ridgway,** born 1759 in Stratton Audley, Oxford. The son of **Pilgrim Ridgeway** and **Sarah Bull**. He married **Elizabeth**.

Children of Pilgrim Ridgway and Elizabeth are:

1.  Mary Ridgeway, born 1789 in Baptised Waddesden 1 May 1789.

2.  Elizabeth Ridgeway, born 1791 in Buckinghamshire Baptised Waddesden 2 June 1793; died after 1851; married John Raven 10 April 1814 in Puttenham Hertford.

3. Thomas Ridgeway, born 1791 Baptised Waddesden 22 June 1791.

4. William Ridgeway, born 1796 Baptised Waddesden 29 May 1796.

5. Dinah Ridgeway, born 1798 Baptised Waddesden 2 September 1798.

6. John Ridgeway, born 1800 Baptised Waddesden 18 May 1800; died before 1803.

7. John Ridgeway, born 1803 Baptised Waddesden 19 June 1803.

**Thomas Dunsford** He married **Eliza**.

Children of Thomas Dunsford and Eliza are:

1. Mary Dunsford, born 1747 Baptised 12 July 1747 St Thomas the Apostle Exeter.

2. James Dunsford, born 1749 Baptised 30 January 1749 St Thomas the Apostle Exeter; married Bridget Burn 27 May 1780 in Okham, Surrey.

3. Thomas Dunsford, born 1753 Baptised 17 February 1753 St Thomas the Apostle Exeter.

4. John Dunsford, born 1756 Baptised 31 July 1756 St Thomas the Apostle Exeter; died 3 August 1756 in Exeter.

# GENERATION NO. 11

**John Gass** He married **Martha**.

Child of John Gass and Martha is:

1. John Gass, born 1756 Baptised 4 April 1756, St Luke Finsbury; married Elizabeth Workman 12 September 1781 in St Dunstan, Stepney.

**William Shildrick,** born 12 June 1726 in Bottisham, Cambridge. The son of **Robert Shildracke** and **Elizabeth Gorzham**. He married **Avis Mott** 30 October 1753 in Bottisham, Cambridge.
**Avis Mott,** born circa 1730. The daughter of **Thomas Mott** and **Sarah**.

Children of William Shildrick and Avis Mott are:

1. John Shildrick, born 1754 in Bottisham Cambridge. Baptised 2 June 1754; died 1808 in Bottisham Cambridge; married Sarah Dilliston 12 November 1776 in Bottisham, Cambridge.

2. Elizabeth Shildrick, born 1756 in Bottisham Cambridge. Baptised 14 June 1756; married Benjamin Hart 22 January 1778 in Bottisham, Cambridge.

3. William Shildrick, born 1770 in Bottisham Cambridge. Baptised 28 October 1770; died 1822 in Buried in Holy Trinity Bottisham Cambridge; married (1) Sarah Flack 7 March 1799 in Bottisham, Cambridge; married (2) Sarah Newman 21 July 1814 in Bottisham, Cambridge.

**Richard Hart.** He married **Margaret Newman** 14 February 1747/48 in Bottisham, Cambridge.

Child of Richard Hart and Margaret Newman is:

1. William Hart, born 22 May 1749 in Bottisham Cambridge; died 23 May 1775 in Stow Cum Quy Cambridge; married Sarah Tuck.

**Thomas Tuck** He married **Margaret.**

Child of Thomas Tuck and Margaret is:

1. Sarah Tuck, born 16 February 1752 in Stow Cum Quy Cambridge; married William Hart.

**Thomas Raven,** born 1729 in Waddesden Buckinghamshire Baptised 25 May 1729. The son of **Joseph Reauing** and **Anne**. He married **Katherine.**

Children of Thomas Raven and Katherine are:

1. Ann Raven, born 1749 in Waddesden Buckinghamshire Baptised 25 Sep 1749.

2. John Wallington Raven, born 1753 in Waddesden Buckinghamshire Baptised 15 July 1753; died 1790 in Waddesden Buckinghamshire; married Joyce Bridges 28 May 1776 in Waddesden.

3.  Archer Raven, born 1759 Baptised May 26th 1759 Waddesden Buckinghamshire.

4.  Alice Kingham Raven, born 1760 in Waddesden Buckinghamshire Baptised 14 Sep 1760.

5.  Diana Raven, born 1763 in Waddesden Buckinghamshire Baptised 16 September 1763.

6.  Sarah Raven, born 1765 in Waddesden Buckinghamshire Baptised 9 November 1765.

**Pilgrim Ridgeway.** He married **Sarah Bull** 13 January 1755 in Upper Winchendon.

Child of Pilgrim Ridgeway and Sarah Bull is:

1.  Pilgrim Ridgway, born 1759 in Stratton Audley, Oxford; married Elizabeth.

# GENERATION NO. 12

**Robert Shildracke,** born 17 November 1696 in Bottisham. The son of **William Shildracke** and **Ann.** He married **Elizabeth Gorzham** 15 September 1725 in Bottisham, Cambridge.

Children of Robert Shildracke and Elizabeth Gorzham are:

1.  William Shildrick, born 12 June 1726 in Bottisham, Cambridge; married Avis Mott 30 October 1753 in Bottisham, Cambridge.

2.  John Shildrake, born 12 September 1731.

3.  Robert Shildrick, born 29 August 1736.

**Thomas Mott,** born February 1705/06 in Bottisham Cambridge. The son of **William Mott** and **Elizabeth.** He married **Sarah.**

Children of Thomas Mott and Sarah are:

1.  Avis Mott, born circa 1730; married William Shildrick 30 October 1753 in Bottisham, Cambridge.

2.  William Mott, born 23 September 1738 in Bottisham Cambridge; married Sarah Bondel 10 October 1764 in Bottisham, Cambridge.

**Joseph Reauing,** born circa 1705. The son of **John Rauen** and **Joane Nebb**. He married **Anne**.

Child of Joseph Reauing and Anne is:

1.  Thomas Raven, born 1729 in Waddesden Buckinghamshire Baptised 25 May 1729; married Katherine.

# *GENERATION NO. 13*

**William Shildracke,** born circa 1660. He married **Ann**.

Children of William Shildracke and Ann are:

1.  Ann Shildrick, born 7 April 1684.

2.  Mary Shildrick, born 25 March 1691; married Benjamin Lawsell 26 March 1722 in Bottisham, Cambridge.

3.  Henry Sheldrake, born 28 January 1692/93.

4.  Robert Shildracke, born 17 November 1696 in Bottisham; married Elizabeth Gorzham 15 September 1725 in Bottisham, Cambridge.

5.  John Sheldrake, born 5 November 1699.

**William Mott**. He married **Elizabeth**.

Child of William Mott and Elizabeth is:

1.  Thomas Mott, born February 1705/06 in Bottisham Cambridge; married Sarah.

**John Rauen,** born circa 1670. The son of **Thomas Raven**. He married **Joane Nebb** 10 October 1691 in Waddesden Buckinghamshire. **Joane Nebb,** born circa 1670.

Children of John Rauen and Joane Nebb are:

1.  John Rauen, born 1694 in Waddesden Buckinghamshire Baptised 24 Aug 1694.

2.  Samuel Rauen, born 1696 in Waddesden Buckinghamshire Baptised 14 June 1696.

3.  Thomas Raven, born 1698 in Waddesden Buckinghamshire Baptised 20 November 1698.

4.  Elizabeth Rauen, born 1704 in Waddesden Buckinghamshire Baptised 8 March 1704.

5.  Joseph Reauing, born circa 1705; married Anne.

6.  William Rauen, born 1706 in Waddesden Buckinghamshire Baptised 2 February 1706; married Elisabeth.

7.  Robert Rauen, born 1709 in Waddesden Buckinghamshire.

8.  Ralph Rauen, born 1711 in Waddesden Buckinghamshire Baptised 25 December 1711.

## GENERATION NO. 14

**Thomas Raven,** born 1653 in Waddesden Buckinghamshire Baptised 25 May 1653. The son of **Joseph Raven** and **Ann**.

Child of Thomas Raven is:

1.  John Rauen, born circa 1670; married Joane Nebb 10 October 1691 in Waddesden Buckinghamshire.

## GENERATION NO. 15

**Joseph Raven,** born circa 1630. He married **Ann**. born circa 1630.

Child of Joseph Raven and Ann is:

1.  Thomas Raven, born 1653 in Waddesden Buckinghamshire Baptised 25 May 1653.

# *About the Author*

Born in Edgware, Middlesex, Sandra Wynn has spent many years working together with her husband building up their successful English language school and travelling all over the world. After recovering from a serious car accident in 2000, she decided to work part-time concentrating only on the international marketing, which gave her the time to fulfil her ambition of writing a book. She has two adult sons and lives happily in Eastbourne with her husband Bob, commuting regularly to Spain to visit her granddaughter.

0-595-28291-1

www.ingramcontent.com/pod-product-compliance
Lightning Source LLC
Chambersburg PA
CBHW031321290526
45784CB00014B/420